the greatest *American* speeches

the greatest American

speeches

the stories and transcripts of the
words that changed our history

Quercus

Quercus Publishing Ltd
46 Dorset Street
London
W1U 7NB

First published 2006
Copyright © Quercus Publishing Ltd 2006

A catalogue record for this book is available from the British Library.

ISBN 1 905204 37 X

Printed in Singapore

Research, compilation, editing and picture research by the Cambridge Editorial Partnership, Michael Young Centre, Purbeck Road, Cambridge CB2 2PF, with thanks to Martin Hall, Carol Schaessens, and Martin Walters. Designed by Zoe Naylor.

Introduction

This book brings together the greatest American speeches, tracing the birth and growth of a still-young nation in the words of its leaders and citizens. It tells the stories of why the speeches were given and how they became so important.

Any selection of this kind is essentially subjective, and every reader will have his or her ideas about what should have been included—or omitted. The speeches here have been chosen for their lasting relevance. Most are from recent history, although some of the greatest date from long before the age of broadcasting. While the majority are by prominent public and political figures, there are many from ordinary citizens—abolitionists, feminists, artists, sportsmen, and innovators—all giving voice to the issues, struggles and achievements of their times. There are speeches that mark critical events, like the bombing of Pearl Harbor, or the terrorist outrages of 11 September 2001. There are studied pieces of oratory from George Washington, John F. Kennedy, and Martin Luther King Jr; personal testimony from Lou Gehrig and Elie Wiesel; words of solemn simplicity from Ronald Reagan; eloquent passion from Frederick Douglass; and addresses given with irresistible spontaneity by General Patton and Robert F. Kennedy.

Radio and television enable a speaker to address an entire nation at the same moment, and the impact of a speech can be assessed almost instantly. In the past, both reception and response were localized and limited—but slower means of communication allowed time for reflection. Abraham Lincoln's audience at Gettysburg were distinctly unimpressed by the reedy-voiced President's three-minute address, yet within days the printed version of his speech was acknowledged as one of the greatest in American history, and is still considered so today. By contrast, modern media are unforgiving of mistakes, hesitation and poor delivery. When Neil Armstrong stumbled over his carefully-rehearsed lines as he took his first step on the moon, tongues tutted all round the world. However, his words are still quoted verbatim, mistake and all: the occasion upstaged the speaker and provided all the meaning for what he said.

Written versions of speeches frequently differ from the words spoken at the time. Extemporizations are often lost, and some speakers cannot resist improving written versions after the event. We are dependent on historical documents and transcripts where original sources are unavailable and all these produce variations. A biographer's account of Sojourner Truth's passionate speech is not as authentic a source as, for example, recorded transmission of Gerald Ford's pardon of Richard Nixon, broadcast live on television.

While some speakers are brief and to-the-point, others talk for hours. Where possible, speeches have been included in their entirety, but some of exceptional duration have had to be edited. Where this has been necessary, the most significant sections remain intact.

Thomas Jefferson, who appears in this book, although he much preferred writing to speaking, stated, "Speeches that are measured by the hour will die with the hour." All the speeches in this collection have stood the test of time.

Contents

"There is a twofold liberty, natural...and civil or federal."

John Winthrop

Acquittal speech before the General Court of the
Massachusetts Bay Colony, 1645

The Puritan settlers who arrived in Massachusetts on 12 June 1630 had left England in search of a life where they could practice their religious beliefs without persecution and build a completely new Christian society. The success of this radical social experiment was due to their leader, John Winthrop, who impressed upon his fellow colonists the need to accept group discipline and individual responsibility. Winthrop thought this new land was best ruled by a small number of educated and devout men, who, he believed, were appointed by God to maintain law.

Before they left England, Winthrop preached his famous sermon, "A Model of Christian Charity," in which he cautioned the Massachusetts Bay colonists that "we shall be as a city upon a hill. The eyes of all people are upon us." If their venture failed, he warned, "we shall be made a story and a by-word throughout the world."

Born into a wealthy, land-owning family, Winthrop was a member of the English ruling class. He studied law at Cambridge University and gained a government post. From his youth he was highly religious, his Puritan beliefs reinforcing his elitist world-view and giving him an urgent desire to improve the "wicked world." An economic slump in England, together with anti-Puritan policies that cost him his job at court, led Winthrop to accept the task of setting up a colony in what the English called the New World.

Born 22 January 1588 in Edwardston, Suffolk, England.
Winthrop's speech on liberty was given on his acquittal on charges of having exceeded his authority as a magistrate. The speech was described by a contemporary historian, James Grahame, as recalling "the most interesting scenes of Greek and Roman history; while, in the wisdom, piety and dignity that it breathes, it resembles the magnanimous vindication of a judge of Israel."
Died 26 March 1649 in Boston, Massachusetts.

Elected Governor before the colonists left England, Winthrop was re-elected numerous times. As a moderate, he struggled against the excesses of radical Puritanism, limiting the number of executions for heresy and blocking oppressive innovations, like forcing women to wear a veil. As dissident Puritan groups gradually split away from the original colony and moved to settle other areas, Winthrop became regarded as the protector of orthodox Puritanism—his own community, he believed, was favored by God above all others.

However, tensions developed over the extent of his authority and in 1645 led to accusations that he had exceeded his power. Winthrop and other magistrates were impeached following an incident in which people believed that they had involved themselves unnecessarily in a local election. After a three-month dispute, Winthrop was acquitted and made his "little speech," in which he defined his political philosophy: broad authority for magistrates and narrow liberty for the people—a limited democracy.

Married four times, Winthrop had at least 15 children and died of natural causes at the age of 61. President Ronald Reagan evoked Winthrop's vision of a new land of freedom, his "city on a hill," in his own farewell speech on leaving office in 1989.

The great questions that have troubled the country are about the authority of the magistrates and the liberty of the people. It is yourselves who have called us to this office, and, being called by you, we have our authority from God, in way of an ordinance, such as hath the image of God eminently stamped upon it, the contempt and violation whereof hath been vindicated with examples of divine vengeance. I entreat you to consider that, when you choose magistrates, you take them from among yourselves, men subject to like passions as you are.

"We account him a good servant who breaks not his covenant."

Therefore, when you see infirmities in us, you should reflect upon your own, and that would make you bear the more with us, and not be severe censurers of the failings of your magistrates, when you have continual experience of the like infirmities in yourselves and others. We account him a good servant who breaks not his covenant. The covenant between you and us is the oath you have taken of us, which is to this purpose, that we shall govern you and judge your causes by the rules of God's laws and our own, according to our best skill. When you agree with a workman to build you a ship or house, he undertakes as well for his skill as for his faithfulness, for it is his profession, and you pay him for both. But, when you call one to be a magistrate, he doth not profess nor undertake to have sufficient skill for that office, nor can you furnish him with gifts, therefore you must run the hazard of his skill and ability. But if he fail in faithfulness, which by his oath he is bound unto, that he must answer for. If it fall out that the case be clear to common apprehension, and the rule clear also, if he transgress here, the error is not in the skill, but in the evil of the will: it must be required of him. But if the case be doubtful, or the rule doubtful, to men of such understanding and parts as your magistrates are, if your magistrates should err here, yourselves must bear it.

For the other point concerning liberty, I observe a great mistake in the country about that. There is a twofold liberty, natural—I mean as our nature is now corrupt—and civil or federal. The first is common to man with beasts and other creatures. By this, man as he stands in relation to man simply, hath liberty to do what he lists: it is a liberty to evil as well as to good. This liberty is incompatible and inconsistent with authority, and cannot endure the least restraint of the most just authority.

...The other kind of liberty I call civil or federal. It may also be termed moral, in reference to the covenant between God and man, in the moral law, and the politic covenants and constitutions, amongst men themselves. This liberty is the proper end and object of authority, and cannot subsist without it. And it is a liberty to that only which is good, just, and honest. This liberty you are to stand for, with the hazard not only of your goods, but of your lives, if need be. Whatsoever crosseth this is not authority, but a distemper thereof. This liberty is maintained and exercised in a way of subjection to authority; it is of the same kind of liberty wherewith Christ hath made us free. The woman's own choice makes such a man her husband. Yet, being so chosen, he is her lord, and she is to be subject to him, yet in a way of liberty, not of bondage; and a true wife accounts her subjection her honor and freedom, and would not think her condition safe and free but in her subjection to her husband's authority. Such is the liberty of the church under the authority of Christ, her king and husband ...

"Quietly and cheerfully submit unto that authority which is set over you."

... On the other side, ye know who they are that complain of this yoke and say, let us break their bands, etc., we will not have this man to rule over us. Even so, brethren, it will be between you and your magistrates. If you stand for your natural corrupt liberties, and will do what is good in your own eyes, you will not endure the least weight of authority, but will murmur, and oppose, and be always striving to shake off that yoke. But if you will be satisfied to enjoy such civil and lawful liberties, such as Christ allows you, then will you quietly and cheerfully submit unto that authority which is set over you, in all the administrations of it, for your good. Wherein, if we fail at any time, we hope we shall be willing, by God's assistance, to hearken to good advice from any of you, or in any other way of God. So shall your liberties be preserved, in upholding the honor and power of authority amongst you.

"Give me liberty or give me death."

Patrick Henry

Speech to the second Virginia Convention, 23 March 1775

In the late eighteenth century, British colonies in North America faced taxes levied by the British government to pay for the British army resident in America. The colonists fiercely resisted this, on the grounds that they should not be taxed by a parliament in which they were not represented. In 1773 the famous Boston Tea Party protest was crushed by the British, kindling further rebellion and leading to the Revolutionary War (1776–83). The "liberty" speech that Patrick Henry gave in 1775 marked the start of the revolt against the British in Virginia.

The man who was later to be called the "Voice of the Revolution" was taught at home by his well-educated Scots father, who gave him a grounding in the classics. After trying unsuccessfully to earn a living as a store-keeper and a farmer, Henry decided to study law in order to provide for his growing family. His talent quickly became apparent and he was admitted to the Bar at the age of 24, building a thriving criminal law practice.

Henry's remarkable oratory, and his willingness to risk charges of treachery toward Britain, first brought him to public attention in the Parson's Cause trial (1763). This trial centered on whether the price of tobacco (which formed the wages of clerymen) should be regulated by the colonial government or the British king. In his eloquent defense, Henry cited the "doctrine of natural rights," a political theory arguing that humans have certain indisputable rights at birth. He won the case, much to the dismay of the British government.

Born 29 May 1736 in Studley, Virginia. With his outstanding oratorical, intellectual, and legal skills, Patrick Henry was a leading figure in the struggle for self-government. In 1775 his fiery speech in St John's Church, Richmond, persuaded the deeply divided Virginia Convention to equip the militia and defend themselves against advancing British forces. The speech guaranteed Henry a place in history as one of the great proponents of liberty. Two counties are named after him, in Alabama and Tennessee.
Died 6 June 1799 in Red Hill Plantation, Virginia.

Following the 1775 "liberty" speech for which he is best known, Henry became war-time Governor of Virginia. He played a prominent role in the 1776 convention and was the first Governor of the Commonwealth under its new constitution. He was, however, a strong anti-federalist opponent of the United States Constitution and worked for the adoption of the Bill of Rights, to ensure the protection of fundamental personal liberties.

Henry served in public office in Virginia for nearly 30 years. Having been persuaded by George Washington to stand for the state legislature in 1799, he gave his last speech at 63—a few months before his death—when, ailing and bent with age, he made a patriotic appeal for unity to preserve the young American republic.

Mr President, it is natural to man to indulge in the illusions of hope. We are apt to shut our eyes against a painful truth, and listen to the song of that siren till she transforms us into beasts. Is this the part of wise men, engaged in a great and arduous struggle for liberty? Are we disposed to be of the number of those who, having eyes, see not, and, having ears, hear not, the things which so nearly concern their temporal salvation? For my part, whatever anguish of spirit it may cost, I am willing to know the whole truth; to know the worst, and to provide for it.

I have but one lamp by which my feet are guided, and that is the lamp of experience. I know of no way of judging of the future but by the past. And judging by the past, I wish to know what there has been in the conduct of the British ministry for the last ten years to justify those hopes with which gentlemen have been pleased to solace themselves and the House. Is it that insidious smile with which our petition has been lately received? Trust it not, sir; it will prove a snare to your feet. Suffer not yourselves to be betrayed with a kiss. Ask yourselves how this gracious reception of our petition comports with those warlike preparations which cover our waters and darken our land. Are fleets and armies necessary to a work of love and reconciliation? Have we shown ourselves so unwilling to be reconciled that force must be called in to win back our love? Let us not deceive ourselves, sir. These are the implements of war and subjugation; the last arguments to which kings resort. I ask gentlemen, sir, what means this martial array, if its purpose be not to force us to submission? Can gentlemen assign any other possible motive for it? Has Great Britain any enemy, in this quarter of the world, to call for all this accumulation of navies and armies? No, sir, she has none. They are meant for us. They can be meant for no other. They are sent over to bind and rivet upon us those chains which the British ministry have been so long forging.

"Our chains are forged! Their clanking may be heard on the plains of Boston!"

And what have we to oppose to them? Shall we try argument? Sir, we have been trying that for the last ten years. Have we anything new to offer upon the subject? Nothing. We have held the subject up in every light of which it is capable, but it has been all in vain. Shall we resort to entreaty and humble supplication? What terms shall we find which have not been already exhausted? Let us not, I beseech you, sir, deceive ourselves.

… There is no longer any room for hope. If we wish to be free, if we mean to preserve inviolate those inestimable privileges for which we have been so long contending, if we mean not basely to abandon the noble struggle in which we have been so long engaged, and which we have pledged ourselves never to abandon until the glorious object of our contest shall be obtained, we must fight! I repeat it, sir, we must fight! An appeal to arms and to the God of hosts is all that is left us!

"Why stand we here idle?"

They tell us, sir, that we are weak; unable to cope with so formidable an adversary. But when shall we be stronger? Will it be the next week, or the next year? Will it be when we are totally disarmed, and when a British guard shall be stationed in every house? Shall we gather strength by irresolution and inaction? Shall we acquire the means of effectual resistance by lying supinely on our backs and hugging the delusive phantom of hope, until our enemies shall have bound us hand and foot? Sir, we are not weak if we make a proper use of those means which the God of nature hath placed in our power. The millions of people, armed in the holy cause of liberty, and in such a country as that which we possess, are invincible by any force which our enemy can send against us. Besides, sir, we shall not fight our battles alone. There is a just God who presides over the destinies of nations, and who will raise up friends to fight our battles for us. The battle, sir, is not to the strong alone. It is to the vigilant, the active, the brave. Besides, sir, we have no election. If we were base enough to desire it, it is now too late to retire from the contest. There is no retreat but in submission and slavery! Our chains are forged! Their clanking may be heard on the plains of Boston! The war is inevitable and let it come! I repeat it, sir, let it come.

It is in vain, sir, to extenuate the matter. Gentlemen may cry, "Peace, peace!" but there is no peace. The war is actually begun! The next gale that sweeps from the north will bring to our ears the clash of resounding arms! Our brethren are already in the field! Why stand we here idle? What is it that gentlemen wish? What would they have? Is life so dear, or peace so sweet, as to be purchased at the price of chains and slavery? Forbid it, Almighty God! I know not what course others may take; but as for me, give me liberty or give me death!

"I agree to this Constitution for all its faults."

Benjamin Franklin

Speech at the Constitutional Convention, Pennsylvania, 17 September 1787

The Treaty of Paris in 1783 ended the War of Independence between Britain and 13 American colonies, which were then established as independent states. One of the signatories was Benjamin Franklin, the only founding father of America to sign the other two major documents that created the United States—the Declaration of Independence and the United States Constitution.

In his early life, Benjamin Franklin was a great admirer of Britain's cultural and literary heritage, and was a respected guest in British social circles. However, he realized that King George III would never willingly cede enough power to the colonies and so, aged 70, Franklin became a radical advocate for American independence. It was his skilled negotiations with France in 1776 that gained America crucial French support in the War of Independence.

At the end of the war Franklin returned to America, where he campaigned for the abolition of slavery and was three times elected President of Pennsylvania's Executive Council. In Pennsylvania, Franklin established the city library, police and fire services and an academy that later became a university. He was also involved in the postal services, increasing their efficiency and solvency. In the summer of 1787, although retired, Franklin was sent as the Pennsylvanian delegate to the Constitutional Convention where he attended daily sessions. Although he failed to impose his own preference for an executive committee, rather than a President, to lead the state, Franklin put aside his objections and urged his colleagues to do likewise. The Constitution was agreed.

Born 17 January 1706 in Boston, Massachusetts. At the end of a life filled with accomplishments in business, science, journalism, diplomacy, civic service, and political reform, Benjamin Franklin continued to steer the course of American history. Aged 81 and too weak to deliver it himself, Franklin contributed this speech on the last day of the Convention on the wording of the new Constitution. Franklin emphasized that compromise was necessary for the greater good. He asked each member who, like himself, might not completely approve of the Constitution to "doubt a little of his own infallibility" and to sign the document. His motion was carried.

Died 17 April 1790 in Philadelphia, Pennsylvania.

Benjamin Franklin was the fifteenth child of a candle and soap maker. He grew up in a humble but pious Protestant household, received little formal education and was apprenticed to one of his brothers as a printer at age 10. He educated himself as a writer and scientist and became a successful businessman, publishing the *Pennsylvanian Gazette* and the annual *Poor Richard's Almanac*, a popular collection of wit and wisdom. He was also an inventor, devising the fuel-saving Franklin stove, the lightning conductor, and bifocal glasses. His contribution to the understanding of electricity was internationally acknowledged.

A national hero and outstanding statesman, Franklin died at the age of 84. His funeral was attended by 20,000 people. In his will, he left the cities of Boston and Philadelphia money in trust for 200 years. The trusts amounted to $7 million when they ended in 1990 and financed major educational projects in both cities.

I confess that there are several parts of this Constitution which I do not at present approve, but I am not sure I shall never approve them. For having lived long, I have experienced many instances of being obliged by better information, or fuller consideration, to change opinions even on important subjects, which I once thought right, but found to be otherwise. It is therefore that the older I grow, the more apt I am to doubt my own judgment, and to pay more respect to the judgment of others. Most men indeed as well as most sects in religion, think themselves in possession of all truth, and that wherever others differ from them it is so far error. Steele, a Protestant, in a dedication tells the Pope, that the only difference between our churches in their opinions of the certainty of their doctrines is, the Church of Rome is infallible and the Church of England is never in the wrong. But though many private persons think almost as highly of their own infallibility as of that of their sect, few express it so naturally as a certain French lady who, in a dispute with her sister, said , "I don't know how it happens, sister, but I meet with nobody but myself, that's always in the right— *Il n'y a que moi qui a toujours raison."*

"I consent, sir, to this Constitution because I expect no better, and because I am not sure that it is not the best."

In these sentiments, sir, I agree to this Constitution with all its faults, if they are such: because I think a general government necessary for us, and there is no form of government but what may be a blessing to the people if well administered, and believe farther that this is likely to be well administered for a course of years, and can only end in despotism, as other forms have done before it, when the people shall become so corrupted as to need despotic government, being incapable of any other. I doubt too whether any other Convention we can obtain, may be able to make a better Constitution. For when you assemble a number of men to have the advantage of their joint wisdom, you inevitably assemble with those men, all their prejudices, their passions, their errors of opinion, their local interests, and their selfish views. From such an assembly can a perfect production be expected? It therefore astonishes me, sir, to find this system approaching so near to perfection as it does; and I think it will astonish our enemies, who are waiting with confidence to hear that our councils are confounded like those of the builders of Babel; and that our States are on the point of separation, only to meet hereafter for the purpose of cutting one another's throats. Thus I consent, sir, to this Constitution because I expect no better, and because I am not sure that it is not the best. The opinions I have had of its errors, I sacrifice to the public good. I have never whispered a syllable of them abroad. Within these walls they were born, and here they shall die. If every one of us in returning to our constituents were to report the objections he has had to it, and endeavor to gain partisans in support of them, we might prevent its being generally received, and thereby lose all the salutary effects and great advantages resulting naturally in our favor among foreign nations as well as among ourselves, from our real or apparent unanimity. Much of the strength and efficiency of any government in procuring and securing happiness to the people depends on opinion, on the general opinion of the goodness of the government, as well as of the wisdom and integrity of its governors.

> **"I cannot help expressing a wish that every member of the Convention who may still have objections to it, would with me, on this occasion, doubt a little of his own infallibility."**

I hope therefore that for our own sakes as a part of the people, and for the sake of posterity, we shall act heartily and unanimously in recommending this Constitution if approved by Congress and confirmed by the Conventions wherever our influence may extend, and turn our future thoughts and endeavors to the means of having it well administered.

On the whole, sir, I cannot help expressing a wish that every member of the Convention who may still have objections to it, would with me, on this occasion, doubt a little of his own infallibility, and to make manifest our unanimity, put his name to this instrument.

"**A passionate attachment of one nation for another produces a variety of evils.**"

George Washington
Farewell address, 17 September 1796

As the first President of the United States of America, George Washington holds a special place in history. Born on 22 February 1732, the son of a Virginia planter, he became a soldier and saw early action in the French and Indian War (1754–63), the bloodiest war of the eighteenth century.

The years 1759–75 were more peaceful for Washington, who concentrated on managing his land around Mount Vernon and served in the Virginia House of Burgesses. During this period, he and other landowners felt increasingly exploited and restricted by British regulations, and Washington became vocal in his objections.

By the fall of 1760, the British controlled all the North American frontier, and in 1763 France surrendered all her American possessions to Britain and Spain. Conflict between the British and the Native Americans gradually led to worsening relations between England and her colonies and to the War of Independence itself, in which Washington was to play a central role.

In 1774 and 1775, Washington took part in two Continental Congresses held by the colonies against British rule, and in 1775 he became Commander of the Continental Army, raised by the colonists. In July that year he began his involvement in the War of Independence, which was to last six years. It was under his leadership that the colonies eventually triumphed, notably through the decisive battle at Yorktown in 1781.

> Born 22 February 1732 in Virginia.
> Washington found speaking in public difficult. His false teeth required him to keep his jaws clenched, so he rarely spoke for more than ten minutes. Nonetheless, he produced noble rhetoric that invested the presidency with great dignity. His farewell address emphasizes the importance of the new Union for domestic and external security.
> Died 14 December 1799 in Virginia.
> Washington's birthday is a public holiday, celebrated on the third Monday in February.

In 1787, Washington chaired the Philadelphia convention that drafted the American Constitution, and at the end of April 1789 he was elected President, by unanimous vote of the Electoral College, taking his oath of office on the balcony of Federal Hall in New York's Wall Street. He was President for two terms.

As President, Washington concerned himself especially with foreign policy. When hostilities between the French and British flared, he insisted on following a policy of neutrality, rather than siding with either, and his powerful Farewell Address includes a warning against America forming long-term alliances.

In retirement he returned to Mount Vernon and when he died in December 1799 he was mourned by the nation for months.

Friends and fellow-citizens. The period for a new election of a citizen, to administer the executive government of the United States, being not far distant, and the time actually arrived when your thoughts must be employed in designating the person who is to be clothed with that important trust, it appears to me proper, especially as it may conduce to a more distinct expression of the public voice, that I should now apprise you of the resolution I have formed, to decline being considered among the number of those out of whom a choice is to be made ...

... I have the consolation to believe that, while choice and prudence invite me to quit the political scene, patriotism does not forbid it.

... A solicitude for your welfare which cannot end but with my life, and the apprehension of danger, natural to that solicitude, urge me, on an occasion like the present, to offer to your solemn contemplation, and to recommend to your frequent review, some sentiments which are the result of much reflection, of no inconsiderable observation, and which appear to me all-important to the permanency of your felicity as a people. These will be offered to you with the more freedom, as you can only see in them the disinterested warnings of a parting friend, who can possibly have no personal motive to bias his counsel. Nor can I forget, as an encouragement to it, your indulgent reception of my sentiments on a former and not dissimilar occasion.

"Your Union ought to be considered as a main prop of your liberty, and that the love of the one ought to endear to you the preservation of the other."

Interwoven as is the love of liberty with every ligament of your hearts, no recommendation of mine is necessary to fortify or confirm the attachment.

The unity of government, which constitutes you one people, is also now dear to you. It is justly so, for it is a main pillar in the edifice of your real independence, the support of your tranquillity at home, your peace abroad; of your safety; of your prosperity; of that very liberty, which you so highly prize.

... Citizens, by birth or choice, of a common country, that country has a right to concentrate your affections. The name of American, which belongs to you, in your national capacity, must always exalt the just pride of patriotism, more than any appellation derived from local discriminations. With slight shades of difference, you have the same religion, manners, habits, and political principles. You have in a common cause fought and triumphed together; the independence and liberty you possess are the work of joint counsels, and joint efforts, of common dangers, sufferings, and successes.

But these considerations, however powerfully they address themselves to your sensibility, are greatly outweighed by those, which apply more immediately to your interest. Here every portion of our country finds the most commanding motives for carefully guarding and preserving the Union of the whole.

… Your Union ought to be considered as a main prop of your liberty, and that the love of the one ought to endear to you the preservation of the other.

… Observe good faith and justice towards all nations. Cultivate peace and harmony with all. Religion and morality enjoin this conduct; and can it be, that good policy does not equally enjoin it? It will be worthy of a free, enlightened, and, at no distant period, a great nation, to give to mankind the magnanimous and too novel example of a people always guided by an exalted justice and benevolence. Who can doubt, that, in the course of time and things, the fruits of such a plan would richly repay any temporary advantages, which might be lost by a steady adherence to it? Can it be, that providence has not connected the permanent felicity of a nation with its virtue? The experiment, at least, is recommended by every sentiment which ennobles human nature. Alas! Is it rendered impossible by its vices?

… A passionate attachment of one nation for another produces a variety of evils. Sympathy for the favorite nation, facilitating the illusion of an imaginary common interest, in cases where no real common interest exists, and infusing into one the enmities of the other, betrays the former into a participation in the quarrels and wars of the latter, without adequate inducement or justification. It leads also to concessions to the favorite nation of privileges denied to others, which is apt doubly to injure the nation making the concessions; by unnecessarily parting with what ought to have been retained; and by exciting jealousy, ill-will, and a disposition to retaliate, in the parties from whom equal privileges are withheld. And it gives to ambitious, corrupted or deluded citizens who devote themselves to the favorite nation facility to betray or sacrifice the interests of their own country, without odium, sometimes even with popularity; gilding, with the appearances of a virtuous sense of obligation, a commendable deference for public opinion, or a laudable zeal for public good, the base or foolish compliances of ambition, corruption, or infatuation.

… Against the insidious wiles of foreign influence I conjure you to believe me, fellow-citizens, the jealousy of a free people ought to be constantly awake; since history and experience prove, that foreign influence is one of the most baneful foes of republican government. But that jealousy, to be useful, must be impartial; else it becomes the instrument of the very influence to be avoided, instead of a defense against it. Excessive partiality for one foreign nation, and excessive dislike of another, cause those whom they actuate to see danger only on one side, and serve to veil and even second the arts of influence on the other. Real patriots, who may resist the intrigues of the favorite, are liable to become suspected and odious; while its tools and dupes usurp the applause and confidence of the people, to surrender their interests.

… The great rule of conduct for us, in regard to foreign nations, is, in extending our commercial relations, to have with them as little political connection as possible. So far as we have already formed engagements, let them be fulfilled with perfect good faith. Here let us stop.

"Observe good faith and justice towards all nations. Cultivate peace and harmony with all."

Europe has a set of primary interests, which to us have none, or a very remote relation. Hence she must be engaged in frequent controversies, the causes of which are essentially foreign to our concerns. Hence, therefore, it must be unwise in us to implicate ourselves, by artificial ties, in the ordinary vicissitudes of her politics, or the ordinary combinations and collisions of her friendships or enmities.

Our detached and distant situation invites and enables us to pursue a different course. If we remain one people, under an efficient government, the period is not far off, when we may defy material injury from external annoyance; when we may take such an attitude as will cause the neutrality, we may at any time resolve upon, to be scrupulously respected; when belligerent nations, under the impossibility of making acquisitions upon us, will not lightly hazard the giving us provocation; when we may choose peace or war, as our interest, guided by justice, shall counsel.

Why forego the advantages of so peculiar a situation? Why quit our own to stand upon foreign ground? Why, by interweaving our destiny with that of any part of Europe, entangle our peace and prosperity in the toils of European ambition, rivalship, interest, humor, or caprice?

It is our true policy to steer clear of permanent alliances with any portion of the foreign world; so far, I mean, as we are now at liberty to do it; for let me not be understood as capable of patronizing infidelity to existing engagements. I hold the maxim no less applicable to public than to private affairs, that honesty is always the best policy. I repeat it, therefore, let those engagements be observed in their genuine sense. But, in my opinion, it is unnecessary and would be unwise to extend them.

"Europe has a set of primary interests, which to us have none, or a very remote relation."

Taking care always to keep ourselves, by suitable establishments, on a respectable defensive posture, we may safely trust to temporary alliances for extraordinary emergencies.

… Though, in reviewing the incidents of my administration, I am unconscious of intentional error, I am nevertheless too sensible of my defects not to think it probable that I may have committed many errors. Whatever they may be, I fervently beseech the Almighty to avert or mitigate the evils to which they may tend. I shall also carry with me the hope, that my country will never cease to view them with indulgence; and that, after 45 years of my life dedicated to its service with an upright zeal, the faults of incompetent abilities will be consigned to oblivion, as myself must soon be to the mansions of rest.

Relying on its kindness in this as in other things, and actuated by that fervent love towards it, which is so natural to a man, who views it in the native soil of himself and his progenitors for several generations. I anticipate with pleasing expectation that retreat, in which I promise myself to realize, without alloy, the sweet enjoyment of partaking, in the midst of my fellow-citizens, the benign influence of good laws under a free government, the ever favorite object of my heart, and the happy reward, as I trust, of our mutual cares, labors, and dangers.

"**We are all Republicans, we are all Federalists.**"

Thomas Jefferson
Inaugural address, Washington, 4 March 1801

Thomas Jefferson was born on 13 April 1743, in Virginia. His father was a landowning planter and surveyor and his mother belonged to a famous colonial family, the Randolphs.

At the College of William and Mary in Williamsburg, Jefferson studied mathematics, natural sciences, French, Latin, Greek, Spanish, Italian, and Anglo-Saxon. He also played the violin and sang, and was a keen sportsman and rider.

He was admitted to the Bar in 1767, though his legal career was hampered by his weakness as a public speaker. Aware of abuses in the law, he became increasingly interested in politics. Although not excelling in oratory, he crafted his speeches with immense care and intelligence, best exemplified by the famous Declaration of Independence, which he drafted in 1776 at the age of 33 and which was adopted by Congress on 4 July 1776. The bill he wrote establishing religious freedom was enacted in 1786.

Jefferson spent the years 1784 to 1789 in Paris, as Minister to France, and became deeply interested in the events leading up to the French Revolution, an experience that influenced his views of equality and democracy. However, his sympathies with the French Revolution led him into conflict with the US Government and he resigned from the Cabinet in 1793. Two parties then emerged: the Federalists and the Democratic-Republicans. Jefferson became leader of the latter, cleverly positioning himself as able to unite the two factions.

In 1796 he became Vice-President under John Adams, and President in 1801. Re-elected for a second term in 1804, with a large majority, his time in office was praised for its simplicity and vision. He maintained that all people are equally worthy of respect, abolished expensive state balls and ceremonies, reduced the army and navy, and cut government expenses.

Born 13 April 1743 in Shadwell, Virginia. Jefferson's first inaugural address confirmed his intention to find common ground with his political opponents and close the breach between Federalists and Republicans. Jefferson avoided making speeches and dealt with matters in writing wherever possible. He refused to speak to Congress for his first State of the Union address in 1801, writing a letter instead. This started a tradition that lasted until 1917, when President Woodrow Wilson made the first personal address for over a century.

Died 4 July 1826.

Jefferson wrote his own epitaph for his gravestone: "Here was buried Thomas Jefferson, author of the Declaration of American Independence, of the statute of Virginia for religious freedom, and father of the University of Virginia."

He retired from office in March 1809, refusing to be a candidate for re-election, although many urged him to stand again. In his twilight years he devoted himself to establishing the University of Virginia at Charlottesville, planning the buildings, and overseeing the organization. He died on 4 July 1826, the fiftieth anniversary of the Declaration of Independence.

Friends and fellow-citizens. Called upon to undertake the duties of the first executive office of our country, I avail myself of the presence of that portion of my fellow-citizens which is here assembled to express my grateful thanks for the favor with which they have been pleased to look toward me, to declare a sincere consciousness that the task is above my talents, and that I approach it with those anxious and awful presentiments which the greatness of the charge and the weakness of my powers so justly inspire. A rising nation, spread over a wide and fruitful land, traversing all the seas with the rich productions of their industry, engaged in commerce with nations who feel power and forget right, advancing rapidly to destinies beyond the reach of mortal eye. When I contemplate these transcendent objects, and see the honor, the happiness, and the hopes of this beloved country committed to the issue, and the auspices of this day, I shrink from the contemplation, and humble myself before the magnitude of the undertaking. Utterly, indeed, should I despair did not the presence of many whom I here see remind me that in the other high authorities provided by our Constitution I shall find resources of wisdom, of virtue, and of zeal on which to rely under all difficulties. To you, then, gentlemen, who are charged with the sovereign functions of legislation, and to those associated with you, I look with encouragement for that guidance and support which may enable us to steer with safety the vessel in which we are all embarked amidst the conflicting elements of a troubled world.

"I believe this ... the strongest Government on earth."

During the contest of opinion through which we have passed the animation of discussions and of exertions has sometimes worn an aspect which might impose on strangers unused to think freely and to speak and to write what they think; but this being now decided by the voice of the nation, announced according to the rules of the Constitution, all will, of course, arrange themselves under the will of the law, and unite in common efforts for the common good. All, too, will bear in mind this sacred principle, that though the will of the majority is in all cases to prevail, that will to be rightful must be reasonable; that the minority

and arraignment of all abuses at the bar of the public reason; freedom of religion; freedom of the press, and freedom of person under the protection of the habeas corpus, and trial by juries impartially selected. These principles form the bright constellation which has gone before us and guided our steps through an age of revolution and reformation. The wisdom of our sages and blood of our heroes have been devoted to their attainment. They should be the creed of our political faith, the text of civic instruction, the touchstone by which to try the services of those we trust; and should we wander from them in moments of error or of alarm, let us hasten to retrace our steps and to regain the road which alone leads to peace, liberty, and safety.

I repair, then, fellow-citizens, to the post you have assigned me. With experience enough in subordinate offices to have seen the difficulties of this the greatest of all, I have learnt to expect that it will rarely fall to the lot of imperfect man to retire from this station with the reputation and the favor which bring him into it. Without pretensions to that high confidence you reposed in our first and greatest revolutionary character, whose pre-eminent services had entitled him to the first place in his country's love and destined for him the fairest page in the volume of faithful history, I ask so much confidence only as may give firmness and effect to the legal administration of your affairs. I shall often go wrong through defect of judgment. When right, I shall often be thought wrong by those whose positions will not command a view of the whole ground. I ask your indulgence for my own errors, which will never be intentional, and your support against the errors of others, who may condemn what they would not if seen in all its parts. The approbation implied by your suffrage is a great consolation to me for the past, and my future solicitude will be to retain the good opinion of those who have bestowed it in advance, to conciliate that of others by doing them all the good in my power, and to be instrumental to the happiness and freedom of all.

"I shall often go wrong through defect of judgment."

Relying, then, on the patronage of your good will, I advance with obedience to the work, ready to retire from it whenever you become sensible how much better choice it is in your power to make. And may that Infinite Power which rules the destinies of the universe lead our councils to what is best, and give them a favorable issue for your peace and prosperity.

The Monroe Doctrine

James Monroe

Address to Congress, 2 December 1823, Washington

A Republican, James Monroe was elected President in 1817 with a huge majority over a Federalist candidate. His administration was referred to as the "Era of Good Feelings" and Monroe remained popular despite an economic slump and conflict over slavery in Missouri.

Monroe rose to office from modest beginnings on a small Virginian landholding. When he was 16, he attended William and Mary College but left to fight in the War of Independence. He served alongside George Washington, was decorated and promoted for heroism and left the army as a major. In 1780 he took up law under the guidance of Thomas Jefferson, then Governor of Virginia. This marked the start of a close friendship.

After election to the Virginia House of Delegates in 1782, Monroe served in the Continental Congress (1783–6). He was an anti-Federalist and in 1790 was elected to the Senate where, despite vigorously opposing President George Washington, he was made minister to France. When he failed to further Washington's plans there, Monroe was recalled to America. In 1799 Monroe became Governor of Virginia, and was twice re-elected.

Under President Jefferson, Monroe acted as an envoy on further diplomatic negotiations in France, Britain, and Spain. In 1807 he resigned as Governor of Virginia to become Secretary of State under President Madison, a post that brought him the burden of foreign affairs during the War of 1812. In 1814 he was made Secretary of War. When he became President, he was the only head of state to have held two cabinet positions.

Born 28 April 1758 in Westmoreland County, Virginia.

James Monroe, fifth President, made a lasting contribution to foreign policy in his Monroe Doctrine, which stated that further European colonization would not be tolerated, the United States would abstain from involvement in European political affairs, and that European intervention in America would be considered an act of hostility. A fourth principle, added later, was opposition to the transfer of existing colonies from one European power to another. In 1821 the capital of Liberia was named Monrovia, in recognition of Monroe's work in supporting the repatriation of blacks to Africa. Died 4 July 1831 in New York City.

Although Monroe lacked the brilliance of other contemporary statesmen, he was praised by Jefferson, Madison, and Adams, who described him as "a mind sound in its ultimate judgments and firm in its final conclusions." Many attributed Monroe's popularity to his being the last of the War of Independence generation: he continued to wear the outdated knee britches, silk stockings, and cocked hat of those revolutionary times, and admirers said he resembled Washington.

At the end of his presidency, Monroe had to sell his Virginian plantation to pay off debts. The property now forms part of William and Mary College. He died of heart failure and tuberculosis in 1831 and was buried in New York City. His body was later reinterred at Hollywood Cemetery, in Richmond, Virginia.

… The occasion has been judged proper for asserting, as a principle in which the rights and interests of the United States are involved, that the American continents, by the free and independent condition which they have assumed and maintain, are henceforth not to be considered as subjects for future colonization by any European powers.

> "It is only when our rights are invaded or seriously menaced that we resent injuries or make preparation for our defense."

… In the wars of the European powers in matters relating to themselves we have never taken any part, nor does it comport with our policy so to do. It is only when our rights are invaded or seriously menaced that we resent injuries or make preparation for our defense. With the movements in this hemisphere we are of necessity more immediately connected, and by causes which must be obvious to all enlightened and impartial observers. The political system of the allied powers is essentially different in this respect from that of America. This difference proceeds from that which exists in their respective governments; and to the defense of our own, which has been achieved by the loss of so much blood and treasure, and matured by the wisdom of their most enlightened citizens, and under which we have enjoyed unexampled felicity, this whole nation is devoted. We owe it, therefore, to candor and to the amicable relations existing between the United States and those powers, to declare that we should consider any attempt on their part to extend their system to any portion of this hemisphere as dangerous to our peace and safety. With the existing colonies or dependencies of any European power we have not interfered and shall not interfere. But with the governments who have declared their independence and maintained it, and whose independence we have, on great consideration and on just principles, acknowledged, we could not view any interposition for the purpose of oppressing them, or controlling in any other manner their destiny, by any European power in any other light than as the manifestation of an unfriendly disposition toward the United States. In the war between those new governments and Spain we declared our neutrality at the time of their recognition, and to this we have adhered, and shall continue to adhere, provided no change shall occur which, in the judgment of the competent authorities of this government, shall make a corresponding change on the part of the United States indispensable to their security.

> "We should consider any attempt on their part to extend their system to any portion of this hemisphere as dangerous to our peace and safety."

The late events in Spain and Portugal show that Europe is still unsettled. Of this important fact no stronger proof can be adduced than that the allied powers should have thought it proper, on any principle satisfactory to themselves, to have interposed by force in the internal concerns of Spain.

… Our policy in regard to Europe, which was adopted at an early stage of the wars which have so long agitated that quarter of the globe, nevertheless remains the same, which is, not to interfere in the internal concerns of any of its powers; to consider the government de facto as the legitimate government for us; to cultivate friendly relations with it, and to preserve those relations by a frank, firm, and manly policy, meeting in all instances the just claims of every power, submitting to injuries from none. But in regard to those continents circumstances are eminently and conspicuously different. It is impossible that the allied powers should extend their political system to any portion of either continent without endangering our peace and happiness; nor can anyone believe that our southern brethren, if left to themselves, would adopt it of their own accord. It is equally impossible, therefore, that we should behold such interposition in any form with indifference. If we look to the comparative strength and resources of Spain and those new governments, and their distance from each other, it must be obvious that she can never subdue them. It is still the true policy of the United States to leave the parties to themselves, in the hope that other powers will pursue the same course.

The Declaration of Sentiments

Elizabeth Cady Stanton

Address to the First Women's Rights Convention, Seneca Falls, 19 July 1848

drunkenness, licentiousness, gluttony, have been dragged naked before the people, and all their abominations and deformities fully brought to light, yet with idiotic laugh we hug those monsters to our breasts and rush on to destruction. Our churches are multiplying on all sides, our missionary societies, Sunday schools, and prayer meetings and innumerable charitable and reform organizations are all in operation, but still the tide of vice is swelling, and threatens the destruction of everything, and the battlements of righteousness are weak against the raging elements of sin and death.

"The right is ours. Have it, we must. Use it, we will."

Verily, the world waits the coming of some new element, some purifying power, some spirit of mercy and love. The voice of woman has been silenced in the state, the church, and the home, but man cannot fulfill his destiny alone, he cannot redeem his race unaided. There are deep and tender chords of sympathy and love in the hearts of the downfallen and oppressed that woman can touch more skillfully than man.

The world has never yet seen a truly great and virtuous nation, because in the degradation of woman the very fountains of life are poisoned at their source. It is vain to look for silver and gold from mines of copper and lead.

It is the wise mother that has the wise son. So long as your women are slaves you may throw your colleges and churches to the winds. You can't have scholars and saints so long as your mothers are ground to powder between the upper and nether millstone of tyranny and lust. How seldom, now, is a father's pride gratified, his fond hopes realized, in the budding genius of his son!

… We do not expect our path will be strewn with the flowers of popular applause, but over the thorns of bigotry and prejudice will be our way, and on our banners will beat the dark storm clouds of opposition from those who have entrenched themselves behind the stormy bulwarks of custom and authority, and who have fortified their position by every means, holy and unholy. But we will steadfastly abide the result. Unmoved we will bear it aloft. Undauntedly we will unfurl it to the gale, for we know that the storm cannot rend from it a shred, that the electric flash will but more clearly show to us the glorious words inscribed upon it: Equality of Rights.

"And ain't I a woman?"

Sojourner Truth

Speech to the Women's Convention in Akron, Ohio, December 1851

Sojourner Truth began life as Isabella Baumfree, the daughter of slaves. She was a slave herself until the age of 30 and some of her own children were sold into slavery.

Parted from her family at an early age, Isabella passed through the ownership of several slave masters, and between 1810 and 1827 bore several children to a fellow slave, Thomas. In 1827, just before New York State finally abolished slavery, she fled to a farm owned by the Van Wagener family, who later freed her. She then successfully fought a legal battle to free her son Peter who had been unlawfully sold to an Alabama planter.

In 1829 Isabella took her two youngest children to New York City and supported her family with domestic work for 10 years. She came to believe that she was commanded by voices to take the name Sojourner Truth, to leave New York and to preach the message of God's goodness and the brotherhood of man. In 1843 she set out with only a bag of clothes and 20 cents. During her crusade she sang, preached and debated throughout the eastern States at meetings, in churches, and on village streets.

Sojourner dictated her autobiography, *The Narrative of Sojourner Truth: a Northern Slave* to a neighbor, Oliver Gilbert, in 1846 and from then on lived on the proceeds of the sales of the book. During the 1850s she drew large crowds with her dramatic lectures on slavery and suffrage. Although she was not the only ex-slave campaigning for the abolitionist cause during the 1840s and 1850s, she was unique in also speaking for women's rights. Matilda Joslyn Gage, writing in *The History of Woman Suffrage*, gave a dramatic account of Sojourner's extempore speech "And ain't I a woman?" at the Women's Convention in Akron, Ohio in 1851, although some argue that Sojourner Truth never actually spoke at the convention. However, she continued to appear at suffrage gatherings for the rest of her life.

Born c. 1797 in Ulster County, New York State. The tall, gaunt figure of Sojourner Truth was an awesome sight on the podiums at religious, abolitionist, and suffrage conventions during the 1840s. Sojourner spoke with a heavy Dutch accent but her natural eloquence and passion ensured that her message came across. Whether she actually delivered the speech with which she is most strongly identified is a matter of debate. However, her association with these words, as much as their powerful prose and imagery, has guaranteed their lasting power.

Died 26 November 1883 in Battle Creek, Michigan.

In 1997 NASA's Mars Pathfinder robotic rover *Sojourner* was named after her.

During the Civil War, Sojourner carried supplies to African-American volunteer soldiers in the Federal army. In 1864 President Lincoln appointed her to a role counseling former slaves about resettlement and entry to the labor market. When she retired in 1875 she was still campaigning to encourage the migration of freed slaves to Kansas and Missouri and advocating a "negro state." Harriet Beecher Stowe once wrote that Sojourner Truth had, more than any other woman she knew, "the silent and subtle power that we call personal presence."

Well, children, where there is so much racket there must be something out of kilter. I think that 'twixt the negroes of the South and the women at the North, all talking about rights, the white men will be in a fix pretty soon. But what's all this here talking about?

That man over there says that women need to be helped into carriages, and lifted over ditches, and to have the best place everywhere. Nobody ever helps me into carriages, or over mud-puddles, or gives me any best place! And ain't I a woman? Look at me! Look at my arm! I have ploughed and planted, and gathered into barns, and no man could head me! And ain't I a woman? I could work as much and eat as much as a man—when I could get it—and bear the lash as well! And ain't I a woman? I have borne thirteen children, and seen most all sold off to slavery, and when I cried out with my mother's grief, none but Jesus heard me! And ain't I a woman?

> **"I have ploughed and planted, and gathered into barns, and no man could head me! And ain't I a woman?"**

Then they talk about this thing in the head: what's this they call it? [*member of audience: "Intellect"*] That's it, honey. What's that got to do with women's rights or negroes' rights? If my cup won't hold but a pint, and yours holds a quart, wouldn't you be mean not to let me have my little half measure full?

Then that little man in black there, he says women can't have as much rights as men, 'cause Christ wasn't a woman! Where did your Christ come from? Where did your Christ come from? From God and a woman! Man had nothing to do with Him.

If the first woman God ever made was strong enough to turn the world upside down all alone, these women together ought to be able to turn it back, and get it right side up again! And now they is asking to do it, the men better let them.

Obliged to you for hearing me, and now old Sojourner ain't got nothing more to say.

"What to the American slave is your Fourth of July?"

Frederick Douglass

Address to the citizens of Rochester, New York, 4 July 1852

Frederick Douglass was born Frederick Bailey. His mother was a slave but the identity of his white father is unknown. When he was eight he was sent to the household of Hugh Auld in Baltimore. Auld's wife taught him to read but Hugh put a stop to Frederick's education, arguing that if a slave learnt to read he would become dissatisfied with his lot and seek freedom. Douglass continued to educate himself secretly. When he was 15, he was rented out to a local farmer, Edward Covey, a vicious slave breaker. Douglass was nearly crushed psychologically by Covey's beatings but finally fought back, defending himself so effectively that Covey never beat him again.

At 16 Douglass was apprenticed in a shipyard and began to plan his escape. In 1837 he met Anna Murray, whom he later married, a freed African-American who helped him flee to Massachusetts disguised as a seaman. He worked as a laborer there for three years, evading slave hunters by changing his name to Douglass. He attended abolitionist meetings and in 1841 made his first speech at an anti-slavery convention in Nantucket. Douglass was so articulate and persuasive that he was hired as an agent by the Massachusetts Anti-Slavery Society and sent on a six-month countrywide tour.

In 1845 Douglass published his autobiography, *Narrative of the Life of Frederick Douglass, an American Slave.*

Born February 1818, in Maryland.

To mark Independence Day in July 1852, Frederick Douglass was invited to make a speech by local dignitaries in his home town of Rochester, New York. He delivered a passionate invective against the hypocrisy of celebrating the principle of liberty while so many black Americans were still not free to enjoy it.

Died 20 February 1895, in Washington DC. Frederick Douglass is one of 21 exceptional Americans celebrated in the Extra Mile Points of Light Volunteer Pathway in Washington.

It was an instant bestseller, although some doubted its authenticity, claiming that the author was too well-educated to have been a slave. The huge publicity had a negative aspect: friends pointed out that it would attract the attention of Hugh Auld, whose "property" Douglass remained, and persuaded Douglass to leave on a protracted tour of Britain.

In two years Douglass earned enough to purchase his freedom and, on returning to New York, to start his own newspaper, the *North Star*. This became a target for anti-abolitionists. On one occasion a group of men tried to smash the printing press. Douglass pre-empted them by striking the first blow, saying, "You can smash machines, but you can't smash ideas."

During the Civil War and the period of reconstruction that followed, Douglass advocated a gradual approach to abolition, and argued that the Constitution could and should be used in the fight against slavery. These views brought him into conflict with abolitionists like William Garrison, who believed that the Constitution was inherently pro-slavery.

Douglass supported the women's rights movement, and was one of the signatories of the "Declaration of Sentiments" that launched it in 1848. On the death of his first wife, he married the feminist Helen Pitts, a white woman 20 years his junior. The marriage caused public controversy, but the couple were supported by Elizabeth Cady Stanton. In his later years Douglass held several government posts, including US minister to Haiti. He died in Washington in 1895. His home, Cedar Hill, is now the Frederick Douglass National Historic Site.

Fellow-citizens. Pardon me, and allow me to ask, why am I called to speak here today? What have I, or those I represent, to do with your national independence? Are the great principles of political freedom and natural justice, embodied in that Declaration of Independence, extended to us? And am I, therefore, called upon to bring our humble offering to the national altar, and to confess the benefits, and express devout gratitude for the blessings resulting from your independence to us?

"Do you mean, citizens, to mock me, by asking me to speak today?"

Would to God, both for your sakes and ours, that an affirmative answer could be truthfully returned to these questions.

... But such is not the state of the case. I say it with a sad sense of disparity between us. I am not included within the pale of this glorious anniversary. Your high independence only reveals the immeasurable distance between us. The blessings in which you this day rejoice are not enjoyed in common. The rich inheritance of justice, liberty, prosperity, and independence bequeathed by your fathers is shared by you, not by me. The sunlight that brought life and healing to you has brought stripes and death to me. This Fourth of July is yours, not mine. You may rejoice, I must mourn. To drag a man in fetters into the grand illuminated temple of liberty, and call upon him to join you in joyous anthems, were inhuman mockery and sacrilegious irony. Do you mean, citizens, to mock me, by asking me to speak today? If so, there is a parallel to your conduct, and let me warn you, that it is dangerous to copy the example of a nation whose crimes, towering up to heaven, were thrown down by the breath of the Almighty, burying that nation in irrecoverable ruin.

... At a time like this, scorching irony, not convincing argument, is needed. Oh, had I the ability, and could I reach the nation's ear, I would today pour out a fiery stream of biting ridicule, blasting reproach, withering sarcasm, and stern rebuke. For it is not light that is needed, but fire; it is not the gentle shower, but thunder. We need the storm, the whirlwind, and the earthquake. The feeling of the nation must be quickened; the conscience of the nation must be roused; the propriety of the nation must be startled; the hypocrisy of the nation must be exposed; and its crimes against God and man must be denounced.

"For revolting barbarity and shameless hypocrisy, America reigns without a rival."

What to the American slave is your Fourth of July? I answer, a day that reveals to him more than all other days of the year, the gross injustice and cruelty to which he is the constant victim. To him your celebration is a sham; your boasted liberty an unholy license; your national greatness, swelling vanity; your sounds of rejoicing are empty and heartless; your denunciation of tyrants, brass-fronted impudence; your shouts of liberty and equality, hollow mockery; your prayers and hymns, your sermons and thanksgivings, with all your religious parade and solemnity, are to him mere bombast, fraud, deception, impiety, and hypocrisy's thin veil to cover up crimes which would disgrace a nation of savages. There is not a nation of the earth guilty of practices more shocking and bloody than are the people of these United States at this very hour.

Go where you may, search where you will, roam through all the monarchies and despotisms of the old world, travel through South America, search out every abuse and when you have found the last, lay your facts by the side of the everyday practices of this nation, and you will say with me that, for revolting barbarity and shameless hypocrisy, America reigns without a rival.

"I deny everything but what I have all along admitted—the design on my part to free the slaves."

John Brown

Address to the court, Harpers Ferry, Virginia, 2 November 1859

John Brown was the son of a tanner and eventually became one himself, although he originally wanted to be a Congregationalist minister. His education and training for the ministry ended prematurely when repeated eye infections prevented him studying.

Brown subsequently had a variety of jobs. As well as working as a tanner, he was a sheep drover, farmer, and wool merchant, before settling down in New York State, in a mainly black community, on land donated by the anti-slavery philanthropist Gerrit Smith. He came to the conclusion that slavery could only be effectively opposed through direct action, and in 1855 he became leader of a group of anti-slavery forces in the Kansas Territory. On 21 May 1856, a pro-slavery mob attacked the town of Lawrence, and Brown vowed vengeance, leading a raid on a pro-slavery settlement at Pottawatomie Creek, during which five men from the opposing camp were killed.

In 1858 his anti-slavery efforts took a political turn and he established a

Born 9 May 1800 in Torrington, Connecticut. Though relatively short, John Brown's final speech is impressive both for the sincerity of its message and for the politeness of its tone. In it he calmly points out that his sole aim is the honorable one of wishing to free the slaves, with no intention to murder, incite rebellion, or destroy property. He is also magnanimous to his captors, noting that their treatment of him was generous.

Died 2 December 1859, Charles Town, (West) Virginia.

The marching song "John Brown's Body" was adopted by Union troops during the Civil War.

stronghold for escaping slaves in the mountains of Maryland and Virginia, even drawing up a provisional constitution for the people of the United States, with the support, both moral and financial, of Gerrit Smith and other Boston abolitionists.

The crisis point came on 16 October 1859, when Brown headed up an armed band of supporters and captured a federal armory at Harpers Ferry. They took 60 men hostage and hoped to inspire escaped slaves to form an army of liberation to free their enslaved kinsmen. The attempt failed, and two days later they surrendered to the Marines. During the struggle, ten of Brown's followers, including two of his own sons, were killed, and Brown himself was wounded. The court found him guilty of treason against the State, insurrection, and murder, and he was hanged.

He wrote the following words on the day he died: "I, John Brown, am now quite certain that the crimes of this guilty land will never be purged away but with blood. I had, as I now think, vainly flattered myself that without very much bloodshed it might be done."

Some regarded John Brown as little more than a troublemaker and terrorist. There is no doubt that he inspired the anti-slavery movement and probably helped to polarize opinion and hasten the Civil War. But to the oppressed slaves of his day, and to many people since, he was a pioneer of human rights, and a martyr to his cause.

I have, may it please the court, a few words to say. In the first place, I deny everything but what I have all along admitted—the design on my part to free the slaves. I intended certainly to have made a clean thing of that matter, as I did last winter when I went into Missouri and there took slaves without the snapping of a gun on either side, moved them through the country, and finally left them in Canada. I designed to have done the same thing again on a larger scale. That was all I intended. I never did intend murder, or treason, or the destruction of property, or to excite or incite slaves to rebellion, or to make insurrection.

I have another objection, and that is, it is unjust that I should suffer such a penalty. Had I interfered in the manner which I admit, and which I admit has been fairly proved—for I admire the truthfulness and candor of the greater portion of the witnesses who have testified in this case—had I so interfered in behalf of the rich, the powerful, the intelligent, the so-called great, or in behalf of any of their friends—either father, mother, brother, sister, wife, or children, or any of that class—and suffered and sacrificed what I have in this interference, it would have been all right; and every man in this court would have deemed it an act worthy of reward rather than punishment.

> **"I never did intend murder, or treason, or the destruction of property, or to excite or incite slaves to rebellion, or to make insurrection."**

This court acknowledges, as I suppose, the validity of the law of God. I see a book kissed here which I suppose to be the Bible, or at least the New Testament. That teaches me that all things whatsoever I would that men should do to me, I should do even so to them. It teaches me, further, to remember them that are in bonds, as bound with them. I endeavored to act up to that instruction. I say I am yet too young to understand that God is any respecter of persons. I believe that to have interfered as I have done—as I have always freely admitted I have done—in behalf of His despised poor was not wrong, but right. Now, if it is deemed necessary that I should forfeit my life for the furtherance of the ends of justice, and mingle my blood further with the blood of my children and with the blood of millions in this slave country whose rights are disregarded by wicked, cruel, and unjust enactments—I submit. So let it be done!

> **"Now, if it is deemed necessary that I should forfeit my life for the furtherance of the ends of justice—I submit. So let it be done!"**

Let me say one word further. I feel entirely satisfied with the treatment I have received on my trial. Considering all the circumstances it has been more generous than I expected. But I feel no consciousness of guilt. I have stated that from the first what was my intention and what was not. I never had any design against the life of any person, nor any disposition to commit treason, or excite slaves to rebel, or make any general insurrection. I never encouraged any man to do so, but always discouraged any idea of that kind.

> **"I feel no consciousness of guilt."**

Let me say also a word in regard to the statements made by some of those connected with me. I hear it has been stated by some of them that I have induced them to join me. But the contrary is true. I do not say this to injure them, but as regretting their weakness. There is not one of them but joined me of his own accord, and the greater part of them at their own expense. A number of them I never saw, and never had a word of conversation with till the day they came to me, and that was for the purpose I have stated.

Now I have done.

"Four score and seven years ago our fathers brought forth on this continent a new nation..."

Abraham Lincoln
The Gettysburg Address, 19 November 1863

"With malice toward none; with charity for all..."

Second inaugural address, 4 March 1865, Washington

Abraham Lincoln grew up in rural Kentucky and Indiana. He summarized his childhood vividly: "It was a wild region, with many bears and other wild animals still in the woods. There I grew up … Of course when I came of age I did not know much. Still, somehow, I could read, write, and cipher, but that was all." The young Lincoln studied avidly by himself, urged on by his stepmother. As a boy he read widely, including the Bible, *Robinson Crusoe*, *The Pilgrim's Progress*, Aesop's *Fables*, the poetry of Robert Burns, Shakespeare, and books about the history of the United States.

At the age of 21 he teamed up with Denton Offutt, an itinerant trader and storekeeper, who helped him build a flatboat and took it down the Sangamon, Illinois, and Mississippi rivers to New Orleans. In 1831 Offutt employed Lincoln in his store in New Salem. It was undemanding work and Lincoln had ample time to study and read.

He studied law and became more and more interested in politics. In 1832 he became a candidate for the Illinois House of Representatives but the election was interrupted by the Black Hawk Indian War. Lincoln volunteered and served as a captain in one of the Sangamon County companies. However, he saw little action and his short military career seems to have been undistinguished.

> Born 12 February 1809 in Hardin County, Kentucky. The Gettysburg Address was given in commemoration of the three-day Battle of Gettysburg, a turning point in the Civil War, which left over 51,000 casualties. Lincoln's high-pitched voice and habit of gesticulating as he spoke made him a poor public speaker, and his speech at Gettysburg was initially coolly received. However, it has since become regarded as one of the greatest in American history. Lincoln's second inaugural speech was his declared favorite. In it, he urged the nation recovering from the Civil War to look to the future.
> Assassinated 14 April 1865 in Washington.

A subsequent venture as a country storekeeper failed and left Lincoln with debts that took 15 years to settle. In May 1833 he became postmaster of New Salem, and the same year was appointed deputy to the surveyor of Sangamon County.

Lincoln was elected a member of the Illinois House of Representatives in 1834, re-elected in 1836, 1838, and 1840, and served in the post until 1842. In 1858 he ran for Senator, and although he lost, his popularity was enough to win him the Republican nomination for the 1860 presidential campaign. However, only the northern States supported Lincoln. Most of the southern States left the Union after Lincoln's election and formed a rebel government. The resulting civil war overshadowed Lincoln's first presidency.

interest was the object for which the insurgents would rend the Union, even by war; while the government claimed no right to do more than to restrict the territorial enlargement of it.

"Let us strive on to finish the work we are in."

Neither party expected for the war the magnitude or the duration which it has already attained. Neither anticipated that the cause of the conflict might cease with, or even before, the conflict itself should cease. Each looked for an easier triumph, and a result less fundamental and astounding. Both read the same Bible, and pray to the same God, and each invokes his aid against the other. It may seem strange that any men should dare to ask a just God's assistance in wringing their bread from the sweat of other men's faces; but let us judge not, that we be not judged. The prayers of both could not be answered; that of neither has been answered fully.

The Almighty has his own purposes. Woe unto the world because of offenses! For it must needs be that offenses come; but woe to that man by whom the offense cometh. If we shall suppose that American slavery is one of those offenses which, in the providence of God, must needs come, but which, having continued through his appointed time, he now wills to remove, and that he gives to both North and South this terrible war, as the woe due to those by whom the offense came, shall we discern therein any departure from those divine attributes which the believers in a living God always ascribe to him? Fondly do we hope—fervently do we pray—that this mighty scourge of war may speedily pass away. Yet, if God wills that it continue until all the wealth piled by the bondsman's two hundred and fifty years of unrequited toil shall be sunk, and until every drop of blood drawn by the lash shall be paid by another drawn with the sword, as was said three thousand years ago, so still it must be said, The judgments of the Lord are true and righteous altogether.

With malice toward none; with charity for all; with firmness in the right, as God gives us to see the right, let us strive on to finish the work we are in; to bind up the nation's wounds; to care for him who shall have borne the battle, and for his widow, and his orphan—to do all which may achieve and cherish a just and lasting peace among ourselves, and with all nations.

The Battle of Little Bighorn

Crazy Horse

Cheyenne River Reservation, 1881

Crazy Horse was one of the most famous of all Native American leaders. His exploits and brave resistance to white settlers opening up the homelands have become legendary. Tasunkewitko, to give him his true name, was a chief of the Oglala tribe of the Sioux nation. He defiantly repelled incursions by the "white man" into Sioux territory in the northern Great Plains, from about 1865 until his death in 1877. His courage has ensured him a permanent place in western sagas.

Early skirmishes included resisting government plans to build a road to access the goldfields of Montana in 1865. Then in Wyoming he was involved in the massacre of a troop of 80 men commanded by Captain William J. Fetterman in 1866, and the Wagon Box Fight of 1867. In an attempt to defuse such conflicts, reservations were set up for the local tribes under the Second Treaty of Fort Laramie in 1868, but Crazy Horse continued to lead hunting expeditions outside these limits. Tension was raised further when gold prospectors entered a reservation in the Black Hills of Dakota in 1874. Crazy Horse then joined with similarly beleaguered Cheyenne Indians, and on 17 June 1876 attacked General George Crook in southern Montana, forcing his withdrawal.

Born between 1838 and 1840 in Bear Butte, near Rapid City, South Dakota.

Crazy Horse's diary account of the Battle of Little Bighorn, originally accompanied by some 40 of his own illustrations, is fascinating. His staccato style lends the account immediacy and impact. His analysis of the conflict also displays his considerable tactical expertise.

Died 5 September 1877 in Fort Robinson, Nebraska.

A gigantic sculpted figure of Crazy Horse now looks out from a mountain in the Black Hills, Dakota, as a permanent monument to a man widely regarded as the greatest of the Sioux leaders.

In what was to become perhaps his most famous battle, Crazy Horse united his men with the Sioux of Chief Sitting Bull on the banks of the Little Bighorn River. Here, on 25 June 1876, they jointly routed a battalion of soldiers led by Lieutenant Colonel George A. Custer, in a battle ever after referred to as "Custer's Last Stand." In this encounter, Crazy Horse displayed considerable cunning and tactical acumen, making full use of the natural landscape to ambush and defeat Custer's forces.

After this battle, Crazy Horse and his followers returned to their homelands, but were pursued by an army under the command of Colonel Nelson A. Miles. Eventually he and his tribe, much weakened by cold and hunger, surrendered to General Crook in Nebraska on 6 May 1877. Crazy Horse finally met his death on 5 September 1877, at the hands of soldiers who were trying to imprison him in a guardhouse at Fort Robinson.

Five springs ago I, with many Sioux Indians, took down and packed up our tipis and moved from Cheyenne river to the Rosebud river, where we camped a few days; then took down and packed up our lodges and moved to the Little Bighorn river and pitched our lodges with the large camp of Sioux.

… I was a Sioux chief in the council lodge. My lodge was pitched in the center of the camp. The day of the attack I and four women were a short distance from the camp digging wild turnips. Suddenly one of the women attracted my attention to a cloud of dust rising a short distance from camp. I soon saw that the soldiers were charging the camp. To the camp I and the women ran. When I arrived a person told me to hurry to the council lodge. The soldiers charged so quickly we could not talk. We came out of the council lodge and talked in all directions. The Sioux mount horses, take guns, and go fight the soldiers. Women and children mount horses and go, meaning to get out of the way.

Among the soldiers was an officer who rode a horse with four white feet. The Sioux have for a long time fought many brave men of different people, but the Sioux say this officer was the bravest man they had ever fought. I don't know whether this was General Custer or not. Many of the Sioux men that I hear talking tell me it was. I saw this officer in the fight many times, but did not see his body. It has been told me that he was killed by a Santee Indian, who took his horse. This officer wore a large-brimmed hat and a deerskin coat. This officer saved the lives of many soldiers by turning his horse and covering the retreat. Sioux say this officer was the bravest man they ever fought. I saw two officers looking alike, both having long yellowish hair.

"The Sioux did not take a single soldier prisoner, but killed all of them. None were left alive for even a few minutes."

… The day was hot. In a short time the soldiers charged the camp. The soldiers came on the trail made by the Sioux camp in moving, and crossed the Little Bighorn river above where the Sioux crossed, and attacked the lodges of the Uncpapas, farthest up the river. The women and children ran down the Little Bighorn river a short distance into a ravine. The soldiers set fire to the lodges. All the Sioux now charged the soldiers and drove them in confusion across the

Little Bighorn river, which was very rapid, and several soldiers were drowned in it. On a hill the soldiers stopped and the Sioux surrounded them. A Sioux man came and said that a different party of soldiers had all the women and children prisoners. Like a whirlwind the word went around, and the Sioux all heard it and left the soldiers on the hill and went quickly to save the women and children.

From the hill that the soldiers were on to the place where the different soldiers were seen was level ground with the exception of a creek. Sioux thought the soldiers on the hill would charge them in rear, but when they did not the Sioux thought the soldiers on the hill were out of cartridges. As soon as we had killed all the different soldiers the Sioux all went back to kill the soldiers on the hill. All the Sioux watched around the hill on which were the soldiers until a Sioux man came and said many walking soldiers were coming near. The coming of the walking soldiers was the saving of the soldiers on the hill. Sioux cannot fight the walking soldiers, being afraid of them, so the Sioux hurriedly left.

The soldiers charged the Sioux camp about noon. The soldiers were divided, one party charging right into the camp. After driving these soldiers across the river, the Sioux charged the different soldiers below, and drive them in confusion. These soldiers became foolish, many throwing away their guns and raising their hands, saying, "Sioux, pity us; take us prisoners." The Sioux did not take a single soldier prisoner, but killed all of them. None were left alive for even a few minutes. These different soldiers discharged their guns but little. I took a gun and two belts off two dead soldiers; out of one belt two cartridges were gone, out of the other five.

… The soldiers charged the Sioux camp farthest up the river. A short time after the different soldiers charged the village below. While the different soldiers and Sioux were fighting together the Sioux chief said, "Sioux men, go watch soldiers on the hill and prevent their joining the different soldiers." The Sioux men took the clothing off the dead and dressed themselves in it. Among the soldiers were white men who were not soldiers. The Sioux dressed in the soldiers' and white men's clothing fought the soldiers on the hill.

The banks of the Little Bighorn river were high, and the Sioux killed many of the soldiers while crossing. The soldiers on the hill dug up the ground, and the soldiers and Sioux fought at long range, sometimes the Sioux charging close up. The fight continued at long range until a Sioux man saw the walking soldiers coming. When the walking soldiers came near the Sioux became afraid and ran away.

"Great in life, he was surpassingly great in death."

James G. Blaine

Funeral oration for President Garfield, Washington DC, 27 February 1882

James Gillespie Blaine was a prominent and ambitious Republican politician, who almost became President in 1884, losing narrowly to the Democrat Grover Cleveland. He was nicknamed "The Plumed Knight," partly because of his qualities of leadership and the eloquence of his speeches.

Blaine was born in West Brownsville, Pennsylvania on 31 January 1830 and graduated from Washington College in 1847. He taught at the Western Military Institute in Kentucky, before returning to Pennsylvania to study law.

From 1859 to 1862 Blaine served in the Maine House of Representatives, and as a Republican Congressman (1863–76). In 1876 and again in 1880 he was a candidate for the presidential nomination, but was unsuccessful on both occasions. After finally winning the Republican nomination, he narrowly lost the presidential race in 1884. He served as Secretary of State to three Presidents: James A. Garfield and Chester Arthur in 1881, and Benjamin Harrison from 1889 to 1892.

Blaine's most significant political achievement was the creation of the Pan American Congress, of which he was the first president. The main aim of the Congress was to relieve tension between the countries of Latin America, and to prevent wars in the Americas. His book *Twenty Years of Congress* is generally regarded as a brilliant historical work.

This famous speech was delivered in honor of President James A. Garfield, who was assassinated in 1881. The assassin, Charles Guiteau, was a lawyer with a history of mental illness who harbored a grudge against the President for some imagined slight. On 2 July, Blaine was with Garfield at the Washington railroad station, where the President was waiting to board a train to the New Jersey coast for a holiday. Guiteau fired two shots. One grazed Garfield's arm, the other lodged in his body and could not be found. After receiving first aid at the scene, Garfield was moved to the White House. The dying President endured many attempts to remove the lost bullet, but was left with a much larger wound, which became infected. It has been argued that President Garfield was killed not by Charles Guiteau, but by the ineptitude of his own doctors. Eventually Garfield was moved to the New Jersey coast. He lingered in great pain for a further 80 days, dying on 19 September.

Born 31 January 1830, in West Brownsville, Pennsylvania.

James Blaine's oration for President Garfield touched the heart of the nation, and stirred widespread devotion. He painted a picture of Garfield as a man full of goodness and potential, and of the deep sadness of his wife and family, culminating in a moving account of Garfield's final wish to die within sight of the ocean, to which he had been heading when intercepted by his assassin.

Died 27 January 1893, Washington, DC.

Garfield's murder stunned many, not least because the President had healed rifts within the Republican Party and was widely respected, but also because the memory of the assassination of President Lincoln, just 17 years earlier, was still fresh.

James Blaine died in Washington, DC on 27 January 1893, and was buried in Oak Hill Cemetery, later to be reinterred in the Blaine Memorial Park, in Augusta, Maine, in 1920.

For the second time in this generation the great departments of the Government of the United States are assembled in the Hall of Representatives, to do honor to the memory of a murdered President. Lincoln fell at the close of a mighty struggle, in which the passions of men had been deeply stirred. The tragical termination of his great life added but another to the lengthened succession of horrors which had marked so many lintels with the blood of the firstborn. Garfield was slain in a day of peace, when brother had been reconciled to brother, and when anger and hate had been banished from the land.

"Garfield was slain in a day of peace."

Great in life, he was surpassingly great in death. For no cause, in the very frenzy of wantonness and wickedness, by the red hand of murder, he was thrust from the full tide of this world's interest, from its hopes, its aspirations, its victories, into the visible presence of death—and he did not quail. Not alone for one short moment in which, stunned and dazed, he could give up life, hardly aware of its relinquishment, but through days of deadly languor, through weeks of agony, that was not less agony because silently borne, with clear sight and calm courage he looked into his open grave. What blight and ruin met his anguished eyes, whose lips may tell; what brilliant, broken plans, what baffled, high ambitions, what sundering of strong, warm, manhood's friendship, what bitter rending of sweet household ties! Behind him a proud, expectant nation, a great host of sustaining friends, a cherished and happy mother, wearing the full, rich honors of her early toil and tears; the wife of his youth, whose whole life lay in his; the little boys not yet emerged from childhood's day of frolic; the fair young daughter; the sturdy sons just springing into closest companionship, claiming every day and every day rewarding a father's love and care; and in his heart the eager, rejoicing power to meet all demands. And his soul was not shaken. His countrymen were thrilled with instant, profound, and universal sympathy.

"With unfailing tenderness he took leave of life."

Masterful in his mortal weakness, he became the center of a nation's love, enshrined in the prayers of a world. But all the love and all the sympathy could not share with him his suffering. He trod the wine-press alone. With unfaltering front he faced death. With unfailing tenderness he took leave of life. Above the demoniac hiss of the assassin's bullet he heard the voice of God. With simple resignation he bowed to the divine decree.

"In the silence of the receding world he heard the great waves breaking on a further shore."

As the end drew near his early craving for the sea returned. The stately mansion of power had been to him the wearisome hospital of pain, and he begged to be taken from his prison walls, from its oppressive, stifling air, from its homelessness and its hopelessness. Gently, silently, the love of a great people bore the pale sufferer to the longed-for healing of the sea, to live or to die, as God should will, within sight of the heaving billows, within sound of its manifold voices. With a wan, fevered face, tenderly lifted to the cooling breeze, he looked out wistfully upon the ocean's changing wonders; on its far sails; on its restless waves, rolling shoreward to break and die beneath the noonday sun; on the red clouds of evening, arching low to the horizon; on the serene and shining pathway of the star. Let us think that his dying eyes read a mystic meaning, which only the rapt and parting soul may know. Let us believe that in the silence of the receding world he heard the great waves breaking on a further shore and felt already upon his wasted brow the breath of the eternal morning.

"Cast down your bucket where you are."

Booker T. Washington

Speech at the Cotton States and International Exposition,
Atlanta, Georgia, 18 September 1895

With some anxiety, the organizers of the 1895 Cotton States and International Exposition in Atlanta invited a black speaker to address their convention. They chose Booker T. Washington, whose views were conciliatory towards whites, disclaiming any desire for social mixing of the races. Washington proposed a "compromise" that blacks should be guaranteed education and technical training in return for withdrawing from politics.

Washington's views on the future for black Americans were optimistic, if deeply conventional: through hard work, thrift, and self-help blacks could improve their skills and gain acceptance. He urged benefactors to shift support from black liberal arts colleges to vocational schools, believing this was the only way black education could survive in the southern heartland.

Booker Taliaferro Washington was an ex-slave who, as a child, worked mornings and evenings in a salt furnace and coalmine so that he could attend school during the day. He once walked 80 miles to enrol at the Hampton Institute in Virginia, and supported himself by working as a janitor. He became a teacher and later joined the staff at Hampton. When the principal was asked to recommend a white head teacher for a new local black school, he suggested employing Washington instead. The Tuskegee Institute, of which Washington was the first principal, had 400 students and taught practical subjects, including farming, carpentry, and domestic skills, as well as academic subjects.

Born 5 April 1856 in Virginia.
Booker T. Washington became a national figure in September 1895, when he gave his so-called "Atlanta compromise speech." In it he urged blacks to "dignify and glorify common labor," giving an acceptable message to whites in both the South and North. However, many blacks felt his views impeded their political and social progress, and contributed to segregation and discrimination in the South.
Died 14 November 1915 in Tuskegee, Alabama.

After his compromise speech, white politicians were keen to support Washington. He gave lecture tours, was consulted by politicians and had a major say in African-American appointments. But Washington had his critics. His seemingly conservative views led to alienation from other black activists, who felt the submissive demeanor he promoted eroded black pride and self-respect. Ultimately Washington's views were rejected by the twentieth-century civil rights movement, despite his practical achievements in establishing a great many small community schools and educational bodies for black people in the South.

In company Washington rarely let down his guard, always conscious of the need to maintain behavior beyond reproach as a spokesman for his race. Before his death, he was recognized with the award of honorary degrees from Harvard University (1886) and Dartmouth College (1901).

A ship lost at sea for many days suddenly sighted a friendly vessel. From the mast of the unfortunate vessel was seen a signal, "Water, water; we die of thirst!" The answer from the friendly vessel at once came back, "Cast down your bucket where you are." A second time the signal, "Water, water; send us water!" ran up from the distressed vessel, and was answered, "Cast down your bucket where you are." And a third and fourth signal for water was answered, "Cast down your bucket where you are." The captain of the distressed vessel, at last heeding the injunction, cast down his bucket, and it came up full of fresh, sparkling water from the mouth of the Amazon river.

To those of my race who depend on bettering their condition in a foreign land or who underestimate the importance of cultivating friendly relations with the Southern white man, who is their next-door neighbor, I would say, "Cast down your bucket where you are." Cast it down in making friends in every manly way of the people of all races by whom we are surrounded.

> **"In all things that are purely social, we can be as separate as the fingers, yet one as the hand in all things essential to mutual progress."**

Cast it down in agriculture, mechanics, in commerce, in domestic service, and in the professions. And in this connection it is well to bear in mind that whatever other sins the South may be called to bear, when it comes to business, pure and simple, it is in the South that the Negro is given a man's chance in the commercial world, and in nothing is this exposition more eloquent than in emphasizing this chance. Our greatest danger is that in the great leap from slavery to freedom we may overlook the fact that the masses of us are to live by the productions of our hands, and fail to keep in mind that we shall prosper in proportion as we learn to dignify and glorify common labor, and put brains and skill into the common occupations of life; shall prosper in proportion as we learn to draw the line between the superficial and the substantial, the ornamental gewgaws of life and the useful. No race can prosper till it learns that there is as much dignity in tilling a field as in writing a poem. It is at the bottom of life we must begin, and not at the top. Nor should we permit our grievances to overshadow our opportunities.

"We shall constitute one-third and more of the ignorance and crime of the South, or one-third of its intelligence and progress."

To those of the white race who look to the incoming of those of foreign birth and strange tongue and habits for the prosperity of the South, were I permitted I would repeat what I say to my own race, "Cast down your bucket where you are." Cast it down among the eight millions of Negroes whose habits you know, whose fidelity and love you have tested in days when to have proved treacherous meant the ruin of your firesides. Cast down your bucket among these people who have, without strikes and labor wars, tilled your fields, cleared your forests, builded your railroads and cities, and brought forth treasures from the bowels of the earth, and helped make possible this magnificent representation of the progress of the South. Casting down your bucket among my people, helping and encouraging them as you are doing on these grounds, and to education of head, hand, and heart, you will find that they will buy your surplus land, make blossom the waste places in your fields, and run your factories. While doing this, you can be sure in the future, as in the past, that you and your families will be surrounded by the most patient, faithful, law-abiding, and unresentful people that the world has seen. As we have proved our loyalty to you in the past, in nursing your children, watching by the sick-bed of your mothers and fathers, and often following them with tear-dimmed eyes to their graves, so in the future, in our humble way, we shall stand by you with a devotion that no foreigner can approach, ready to lay down our lives, if need be, in defense of yours, interlacing our industrial, commercial, civil, and religious life with yours in a way that shall make the interests of both races one. In all things that are purely social, we can be as separate as the fingers, yet one as the hand in all things essential to mutual progress.

... Nearly sixteen millions of hands will aid you in pulling the load upward, or they will pull against you the load downward. We shall constitute one-third and more of the ignorance and crime of the South, or one-third its intelligence and progress; we shall contribute one-third to the business and industrial prosperity of the South, or we shall prove a veritable body of death, stagnating, depressing, retarding every effort to advance the body politic.

> **"The opportunity to earn a dollar in a factory just now is worth infinitely more than the opportunity to spend a dollar in an opera-house."**

… The wisest among my race understand that the agitation of questions of social equality is the extremist folly, and that progress in the enjoyment of all the privileges that will come to us must be the result of severe and constant struggle rather than of artificial forcing. No race that has anything to contribute to the markets of the world is long in any degree ostracized. It is important and right that all privileges of the law be ours, but it is vastly more important that we be prepared for the exercise of these privileges. The opportunity to earn a dollar in a factory just now is worth infinitely more than the opportunity to spend a dollar in an opera-house. In conclusion, may I repeat that nothing in 30 years has given us more hope and encouragement, and drawn us so near to you of the white race, as this opportunity offered by the exposition; and here bending, as it were, over the altar that represents the results of the struggles of your race and mine, both starting practically empty-handed three decades ago, I pledge that in your effort to work out the great and intricate problem which God has laid at the doors of the South, you shall have at all times the patient, sympathetic help of my race; only let this be constantly in mind, that, while from representations in these buildings of the product of field, of forest, of mine, of factory, letters, and art, much good will come, yet far above and beyond material benefits will be that higher good, that, let us pray God, will come, in a blotting out of sectional differences and racial animosities and suspicions, in a determination to administer absolute justice, in a willing obedience among all classes to the mandates of law. This, coupled with our material prosperity, will bring into our beloved South a new heaven and a new earth.

"The man with the muck rake."

Theodore Roosevelt

Speech at the laying of the corner stone of the Cannon Office Building,
Washington DC, 15 April 1906

Theodore ("Teddy") Roosevelt was the second of four children from a wealthy and prominent family of Anglo-Dutch ancestry. As a child he was frail and asthmatic, and was educated at home by private tutors. After gaining a place at Harvard in 1880, he studied for a short time at Columbia Law School, and became increasingly interested in writing and politics.

Roosevelt started to make a name for himself in politics when he was elected to the New York State Assembly as a Republican at the age of 23. But his budding political career was tragically interrupted by the death of both his mother and first wife on the same day in 1884, two days after the birth of their first child. After this double loss, Roosevelt retired from public life to his cattle ranch in Dakota.

In 1886 Roosevelt began a new phase of life, marrying Edith Kermit Carow, whom he had known since childhood, and the following year he re-entered politics. He became President of the New York City Board of Police Commissioners and Assistant Secretary of the Navy under President William McKinley, who selected him as his Vice-President.

Born 27 October 1858 in New York City. Theodore Roosevelt's famous speech was inspired by John Bunyan's description in *The Pilgrim's Progress* of the man with the muck rake, who was unable to look up from his work and find salvation. Roosevelt pleaded for balance between the detection of evil in society and the ability to recognize what is good and to strive for it.
Died 6 January 1919 in Oyster Bay, New York.

When McKinley was assassinated in September 1901, Roosevelt became President, just short of his forty-third birthday. In 1904 he won a second term with a landslide victory. Roosevelt made the White House the focus of his presidency and a vibrant home for his second and growing family. Here he entertained people from all walks of life, including explorers, artists, writers, prize-fighters, and cowboys. Roosevelt's domestic and foreign achievements were numerous. He increased the power of the Federal Government and weakened the influence of private organizations; introduced the "Square Deal" that regulated the economy; launched national conservation programs; funded the construction of the Panama Canal; and negotiated the end of the Russian-Japanese War (1905). For this, he was awarded the Nobel Peace Prize.

In 1906 Congress passed the Pure Food and Drug and Meat Inspection acts, creating agencies to assure the quality of food and consumer protection. The often squalid conditions of the food processing industries had been exposed by journalists—so-called "muckrakers." In his famous speech of 15 April 1906, Roosevelt cleverly turned the concept against itself to highlight the dangers of hypocrisy and bias in social and political comment.

their expense; which denounces bribery, but blinds itself to blackmail; which foams with rage if a corporation secures favors by improper methods, and merely leers with hideous mirth if the corporation is itself wronged.

The only public servant who can be trusted honestly to protect the rights of the public against the misdeeds of a corporation is that public man who will just as surely protect the corporation itself from wrongful aggression.

If a public man is willing to yield to popular clamor and do wrong to the men of wealth or to rich corporations, it may be set down as certain that if the opportunity comes he will secretly and furtively do wrong to the public in the interest of a corporation.

> "The foundation-stone of national life is, and ever must be, the high individual character of the average citizen."

But in addition to honesty, we need sanity. No honesty will make a public man useful if that man is timid or foolish, if he is a hot-headed zealot or an impracticable visionary. As we strive for reform we find that it is not at all merely the case of a long uphill pull. On the contrary, there is almost as much of breeching work as of collar work. To depend only on traces means that there will soon be a runaway and an upset.

… More important than aught else is the development of the broadest sympathy of man for man. The welfare of the wage worker, the welfare of the tiller of the soil, upon these depend the welfare of the entire country; their good is not to be sought in pulling down others; but their good must be the prime object of all our statesmanship.

Materially we must strive to secure a broader economic opportunity for all men, so that each shall have a better chance to show the stuff of which he is made. Spiritually and ethically we must strive to bring about clean living and right thinking. We appreciate that the things of the body are important; but we appreciate also that the things of the soul are immeasurably more important.

The foundation stone of national life is, and ever must be, the high individual character of the average citizen.

"The world must be made safe for democracy."

Woodrow Wilson

Speech to Congress, 2 April 1917

This speech by President Woodrow Wilson, marked the entry of America into World War I. Up to this point the country had been neutral, although Wilson had actively mediated for peace, since 1914. In 1917 Germany renewed its all-out submarine warfare and, as a result of public opinion and the pressure of world events, Wilson asked Congress to declare war on Germany, a decision passed by a majority.

The son of a Presbyterian minister, Wilson grew up in an academic household and lived his later life by a strict personal code of conduct. After studying law and being admitted to the Bar in 1881, he turned to academia, teaching at Princeton University (where he was elected President) for 12 years. His next move was into Democratic politics, working his way up until he became President in 1913. Wilson strongly believed in the rights of all men and set out to establish equality of opportunity within the country. During his presidency he tried to maintain peaceful relations with foreign countries by avoiding the use of threat or force.

Once America was involved in the war, Wilson worked to influence a peace settlement. In 1918 he presented a 14-point peace plan that brought the Allies and Germans to the bargaining table later that year. Wilson headed the US delegation to the Versailles Peace Conference, where he was greeted as a hero. He was successful in gaining acceptance that a League of Nations should be part of the treaty. However, the nationalistic aspirations of the different countries attending dismayed him and he was forced to make concessions to national, territorial, and economic demands. It was only his shrewd bargaining that prevented harsher terms being imposed on Germany.

Born 28 December 1856 in Virginia. Woodrow Wilson revived the custom, abandoned in 1801, of addressing Congress in person. In his speech to Congress in 1917, he announced that diplomatic relations with Germany were severed and declared that the United States would wage war for liberty and peace.

Part of the speech also expresses the kernel of Wilson's belief in an international organization committed to establishing and maintaining world peace.

Died 3 January 1924 in Washington, DC.

However, Wilson faced opposition to the League at home. His dream of America being part of the League of Nations was never realized, due in part to his own refusal to allow the treaty to be modified. He launched himself on a grueling national tour defending the League and arguing that US membership was essential to lasting world peace, but the strain provoked a stroke in 1919. He continued to oppose restrictions to the League from his bed and viewed the 1920 presidential election as a referendum on the League. The Republican Warren Hardy, an opponent of the League, won by a landslide.

In 1919 Woodrow Wilson was awarded the Nobel Peace Prize, in recognition of his vision of an international organization that would work for world peace.

The present German submarine warfare against commerce is a warfare against mankind. It is war against all nations ... The challenge is to all mankind.

Each nation must decide for itself how it will meet it. The choice we make for ourselves must be made with a moderation of counsel and temperateness of judgment befitting our character and our motives as a nation. We must put excited feeling away. Our motive will not be revenge or the victorious assertion of the physical might of the nation, but only the vindication of right, of human right, of which we are only a single champion.

... Armed neutrality is ineffectual enough at best; in such circumstances and in the face of such pretensions it is worse than ineffectual; it is likely only to produce what it was meant to prevent; it is practically certain to draw us into the war without either the rights or the effectiveness of belligerents. There is one choice we cannot make, we are incapable of making: we will not choose the path of submission and suffer the most sacred rights of our nation and our people to be ignored or violated. The wrongs against which we now array ourselves are no common wrongs: they cut to the very roots of human life.

With a profound sense of the solemn and even tragical character of the step I am taking ... I advise that the Congress declare the recent course of the Imperial German Government to be in fact nothing less than war against the government and people of the United States; that it formally accept the status of belligerent which has thus been thrust upon it; and that it take immediate steps not only to put the country in a more thorough state of defense but also to exert all its power and employ all its resources to bring the Government of the German Empire to terms and end the war.

"It is a fearful thing to lead this great peaceful people into war."

... We should keep constantly in mind the wisdoms of interfering as little as possible in our own preparation and in the equipment of our own military forces with the duty—for it will be a very practical duty—of supplying the nations already at war with Germany with the materials which they can obtain only from us or by our assistance. They are in the field and we should help them in every way to be effective there.

... While we do these things, these deeply momentous things, let us be very clear, and make very clear to all the world what our motives and our objects are ... Our object ... is to vindicate the principles of peace and justice in the life of the world as against selfish and autocratic power and to set up amongst the really free and self-governed peoples of the world such a concert of purpose and of action as will henceforth ensure the observance of those principles.

... A steadfast concert for peace can never be maintained except by a partnership of democratic nations. No autocratic government could be trusted to keep faith within it or observe its covenants. It must be a league of honor, a partnership of opinion.

... The world must be made safe for democracy. Its peace must be planted upon the tested foundations of political liberty. We have no selfish ends to serve.

We desire no conquest, no dominion. We seek no indemnities for ourselves, no material compensation for the sacrifices we shall cheerfully make. We are but one of the champions of the rights of mankind. We shall be satisfied when those rights have been made as secure as the faith and the freedom of nations can make them.

... It is a distressing and oppressive duty, Gentlemen of the Congress, which I have performed in thus addressing you. There are, it may be, many months of fiery trial and sacrifice ahead of us. It is a fearful thing to lead this great peaceful people into war, into the most terrible and disastrous of all wars, civilization itself seeming to be in the balance.

But the right is more precious than peace, and we shall fight for the things which we have always carried nearest our hearts, for democracy, for the right of those who submit to authority to have a voice in their own governments, for the rights and liberties of small nations, for a universal dominion of right by such a concert of free peoples as shall bring peace and safety to all nations and make the world at last free.

To such a task we can dedicate our lives and our fortunes, everything that we are and everything that we have, with the pride of those who know that the day has come when America is privileged to spend her blood and her might for the principles that gave her birth and happiness and the peace which she has treasured. God helping her, she can do no other.

"Now at last we can begin."

Crystal Eastman

Speech at the First Feminist Congress, New York, 1919

him throughout life, and half-consciously he began to cultivate that helplessness until today it is the despair of feminist wives.

… As far as we can see ahead people will always want homes, and a happy home cannot be had without a certain amount of rather monotonous work and responsibility. How can we change the nature of man so that he will honorably share that work and responsibility and thus make the homemaking enterprise a song instead of a burden? Most assuredly not by laws or revolutionary decrees. Perhaps we must cultivate or simulate a little of that highly prized helplessness ourselves. But fundamentally it is a problem of education, of early training: we must bring up feminist sons.

… Birth control is just as elementary an essential in our propaganda as equal pay. Women are to have children when they want them, that's the first thing. That ensures some freedom of occupational choice; those who do not wish to be mothers will not have an undesired occupation thrust upon them by accident, and those who do wish to be mothers may choose in a general way how many years of their lives they will devote to the occupation of child-raising.

"Raising children is peculiarly and directly a service to society."

… That brings us to the fourth feature of our program: motherhood endowment. It seems that the only way we can keep mothers free, at least in a capitalist society, is by the establishment of a principle that the occupation of raising children is peculiarly and directly a service to society, and that the mother upon whom the necessity and privilege of performing this service naturally falls is entitled to an adequate economic reward from the political government. It is idle to talk of real economic independence for women unless this principle is accepted. But with a generous endowment of motherhood provided by legislation, with all laws against voluntary motherhood and education in its methods repealed, with the feminist ideal of education accepted in home and school, and with all special barriers removed in every field of human activity, there is no reason why woman should not become almost a human thing.

It will be time enough then to consider whether she has a soul.

"I believe in the law of love."

Clarence Darrow

Closing speech in defense of Henry Sweet, 11 May 1926

As the growing car industry brought an influx of black workers to Detroit in the early 1920s, racial hatred was stirred up by Ku Klux Klan rallies. White mobs drove out black professionals living in largely white housing areas and threatened others planning to move in. The night the Sweet family moved into their home an organized riot broke out and they reacted by shooting from an upper floor. Leon Breiner, a white man, was killed. The Sweets were then tried for murder as a family and defended by Clarence Darrow. The jury failed to reach a verdict and the defendants were released on bail. Darrow then defended Henry Sweet, who admitted to firing a gun, in the first of individual trials planned for each family member.

In his long summing-up, Darrow argued that the Sweet case was about racism, not murder: "I insist that there is nothing but prejudice in this case; that if it was reversed and 11 white men had shot and killed a black while protecting their home and their lives against a mob of blacks, nobody would have dreamed of having them indicted … Now, that is the case, gentlemen, and that is all there is to this case. Take the hatred away, and you have nothing left." The jury took four hours to reach a "not guilty" verdict and in July 1926 the other defendants' charges were dropped.

Born 18 April 1857 in Kinsman, Ohio. Clarence Darrow left no one who heard him in any doubt of his greatness as a speaker. In this speech, as in many others, he rejected high-flown and grandiose language, relying instead on informality, humor, understatement, and pithy argument to create his effect. Died 13 March 1938 in Chicago, Illinois.

Born in 1857 in rural Ohio, Darrow was admitted to the Bar in 1878 and practiced locally for some years. Inspired by the liberal and progressive ideas of Judge John Altgeld, Darrow moved to Chicago in 1887 where he and Altgeld became friends. Darrow became active in local democratic politics and in 1890 was appointed Chicago's corporation counsel. He specialized initially in labor law and later moved into criminal law, becoming involved in various headline-making cases. These included the Leopold–Loeb case (1924), in which Darrow made innovative and successful use of psychiatric theories about determinism in human behavior to have two teenagers' likely death sentences for murdering a young boy commuted to life imprisonment.

A lifelong agnostic, in 1925 Darrow took on the high-profile but ultimately unsuccessful defense of John Thomas Scopes for violating Tennessee's laws banning the teaching of the theory of evolution in public schools—the Scopes "Monkey" trial. Darrow's cross-examination of the anti-scientific, fundamentalist side won national attention.

Darrow was a prolific writer, speaker, and lecturer. Despising convention, he often appeared in court in shirtsleeves and braces. In more than 50 capital cases he lost only his first client to execution and was a strong opponent of capital punishment. After his death Darrow became a folk hero, the subject of various novels and plays, and still inspires a following in the modern Bar.

Now, gentlemen, just one more word, and I am through with this case. I do not live in Detroit. But I have no feeling against this city. In fact, I shall always have the kindest remembrance of it, especially if this case results as I think and feel that it will. I am the last one to come here to stir up race hatred, or any other hatred. I do not believe in the law of hate. I may not be true to my ideals always, but I believe in the law of love, and I believe you can do nothing with hatred. I would like to see a time when man loves his fellow man, and forgets his color or his creed. We will never be civilized until that time comes.

I know the Negro race has a long road to go. I believe the life of the Negro race has been a life of tragedy, of injustice, of oppression. The law has made him equal, but man has not. And, after all, the last analysis is, what has man done and not what has the law done? I know there is a long road ahead of him, before he can take the place which I believe he should take. I know that before him there is suffering, sorrow, tribulation, and death among the blacks, and perhaps the whites. I am sorry. I would do what I could to avert it. I would advise patience; I would advise toleration; I would advise understanding; I would advise all of those things which are necessary for men who live together. Gentlemen, what do you think is your duty in this case? I have watched, day after day, these black, tense faces that have crowded this court. These black faces that now are looking to you 12 whites, feeling that the hopes and fears of a race are in your keeping.

"I believe you can do nothing with hatred."

This case is about to end, gentlemen. To them, it is life. Not one of their color sits on this jury. Their fate is in the hands of 12 whites. Their eyes are fixed on you, their hearts go out to you, and their hopes hang on your verdict.

This is all. I ask you, on behalf of this defendant, on behalf of these helpless ones who turn to you, and more than that—on behalf of this great state, and this great city which must face this problem, and face it fairly—I ask you, in the name of progress and of the human race, to return a verdict of not guilty in this case.

"The only thing we have to fear is fear itself."

Franklin D. Roosevelt
Inaugural address, 4 March 1933

"A date which will live in infamy."

Speech to Congress, 8 December 1941

Franklin D. Roosevelt was a cousin of President Teddy Roosevelt but belonged to the Democrat branch of the family. He was the only child of an extremely wealthy, philanthropic couple (his father made a fortune in the railroad industry) and grew up with a strong sense of social responsibility despite his privileged upbringing. His early life was dominated by his relationship with his mother, Sara Delano Roosevelt. Unable to have any more children after the birth of Franklin, she made him the focus of her life and her possessive, controlling personality posed difficulties for him throughout his own. He survived her by only four years.

Born 30 January 1882 in New York. Franklin D. Roosevelt's first inaugural speech announced policies that re-established the economy after the Depression. He used language as a powerful political tool and changed forever the way that executive office holders address the nation. Roosevelt preferred plain, direct speech to the kind of rhetoric used by the Presidents who went before him.
Died 12 April 1945 in Warm Springs, Georgia.

After attending law school and working in a Wall Street law firm, Franklin married Anna Eleanor Roosevelt, a distant relative, in 1905. Sara Roosevelt was strongly opposed to his choice of wife and her interference in the Roosevelts' marriage was a constant strain. However, the Roosevelts were financially dependent on Sara and her presence in their household was unavoidable. The couple were established members of New York's high society but also concerned with wider social issues. Handsome, talented, and supported by the Roosevelt name and money, Franklin's entry into politics was straightforward. He won a seat as a Democrat in the New York State Senate in 1910. Between 1913 and 1920 he was Assistant Secretary of the Navy under President Woodrow Wilson.

In 1918, the discovery by Eleanor of his long affair with her social secretary led to the collapse of his marriage. Sara Roosevelt's threat to remove her financial support if the couple divorced was an important factor in their decision to remain together. From this time, the Roosevelts' relationship was one of friends and colleagues. After Franklin contracted polio in 1921, which caused him to be confined to a wheelchair, Eleanor worked with him in his campaigns for the governorship of New York, which he won, and later the vice-presidency and presidency, traveling all over the country on his behalf.

Roosevelt was first elected President in 1932. He ran on the promise "I pledge you, I pledge myself, to a new deal for the American people." His confidence and determination, as well as his New Deal, rallied the country as it struggled to recover from the Great Depression. The now-famous speech he gave at his inauguration, stating that "the only thing we have to fear is fear itself," was a reassuring demonstration of his considerable powers of leadership in a crisis. Roosevelt then expedited a series of new legislation to enable the nation's economic recovery.

Roosevelt's personal popularity did not wane. He was overwhelmingly re-elected President in 1936 and in 1940 won a third term.

This is pre-eminently the time to speak the truth, the whole truth, frankly and boldly. Nor need we shrink from honestly facing conditions in our country today. This great nation will endure as it has endured, will revive and will prosper. So first of all let me assert my firm belief that the only thing we have to fear is fear itself—nameless, unreasoning, unjustified terror which paralyzes needed efforts to convert retreat into advance. In every dark hour of our national life a leadership of frankness and vigor has met with that understanding and support of the people themselves which is essential to victory. I am convinced that you will again give that support to leadership in these critical days.

In such a spirit on my part and on yours we face our common difficulties. They concern, thank God, only material things. Values have shrunken to fantastic levels. Taxes have risen, our ability to pay has fallen, government of all kinds is faced by serious curtailment of income, the means of exchange are frozen in the currents of trade, the withered leaves of industrial enterprise lie on every side, farmers find no markets for their produce, the savings of many years in thousands of families are gone.

More important, a host of unemployed citizens face the grim problem of existence, and an equally great number toil with little return. Only a foolish optimist can deny the dark realities of the moment.

Yet our distress comes from no failure of substance. We are stricken by no plague of locusts. Compared with the perils which our forefathers conquered because they believed and were not afraid, we have still much to be thankful for. Nature still offers her bounty and human efforts have multiplied it. Plenty is at our doorstep, but a generous use of it languishes in the very sight of the supply.

Primarily this is because the rulers of the exchange of mankind's goods have failed, through their own stubbornness and their own incompetence, have admitted their failure, and abdicated. Practices of the unscrupulous moneychangers stand indicted in the court of public opinion, rejected by the hearts and minds of men.

True they have tried, but their efforts have been cast in the pattern of an outworn tradition. Faced by failure of credit they have proposed only the lending of more money. Stripped of the lure of profit by which to induce our people to follow their false leadership, they have resorted to exhortations, pleading tearfully for restored confidence. They know only the rules of a generation of self-seekers. They have no vision, and when there is no vision the people perish.

"When there is no vision the people perish."

The moneychangers have fled from their high seats in the temple of our civilization. We may now restore that temple to the ancient truths. The measure of the restoration lies in the extent to which we apply social values more noble than mere monetary profit.

... Our greatest primary task is to put people to work. This is no unsolvable problem if we face it wisely and courageously. It can be accompanied in part by direct recruiting by the government itself, treating the task as we would treat the emergency of a war, but at the same time, through this employment, accomplishing greatly needed projects to stimulate and reorganize the use of our national resources.

Hand in hand with this, we must frankly recognize the over-balance of population in our industrial centers and, by engaging on a national scale in a redistribution, endeavor to provide a better use of the land for those best fitted for the land.

The task can be helped by definite efforts to raise the values of agricultural products and with this the power to purchase the output of our cities.

It can be helped by preventing realistically the tragedy of the growing loss, through foreclosure, of our small homes and our farms.

It can be helped by insistence that the Federal, State, and local governments act forthwith on the demand that their cost be drastically reduced.

It can be helped by the unifying of relief activities which today are often scattered, uneconomical, and unequal. It can be helped by national planning for, and supervision of, all forms of transportation and of communications and other utilities which have a definitely public character.

There are many ways in which it can be helped, but it can never be helped merely by talking about it. We must act, and act quickly.

… For the trust reposed in me I will return the courage and the devotion that befit the time. I can do no less.

"We must act, and act quickly."

We face the arduous days that lie before us in the warm courage of national unity, with the clear consciousness of seeking old and precious moral values, with the clean satisfaction that comes from the stern performance of duty by old and young alike.

We aim at the assurance of a rounded and permanent national life.

We do not distrust the future of essential democracy. The people of the United States have not failed. In their need they have registered a mandate that they want direct, vigorous action.

They have asked for discipline and direction under leadership. They have made me the present instrument of their wishes. In the spirit of the gift I will take it.

In this dedication of a nation we humbly ask the blessing of God. May He protect each and every one of us! May He guide me in the days to come.

In November 1941 diplomatic negotiations between the US and Japan broke down and, although Japan had not declared war on the US, American spies indicated that Japanese naval forces were moving towards the oil-rich East Indies and Malaya. Reports that aircraft carriers were heading towards Hawaii were not taken seriously.

On 7 December 1941, Japan unexpectedly attacked the Pacific fleet at its base in Pearl Harbor, Hawaii. By noon that day eight battleships had been sunk or disabled and 2,403 servicemen and civilians killed. The next day Roosevelt declared war on Japan. On 11 December Japan's allies, Germany and Italy, declared war against the US.

Once in the war, Roosevelt mobilized industry for military production. Despite his failing health, he undertook strenuous foreign travel to ensure his personal input into diplomatic negotiations between the Allies. He worked with British Prime Minister Winston Churchill to determine military and naval policy and met the Soviet premier Josef Stalin at Tehran in 1943 and Yalta in 1944. In that year he won an unprecedented fourth term as President but, exhausted by the pressures of wartime leadership, died soon afterwards.

After Roosevelt's death, the Twenty-Second Amendment to the Constitution, which limits the time a President can remain in office to two terms, was ratified. Roosevelt is the only President to have served more than 12 years in office. He is now regarded as one of the greatest political figures in American history.

Mr Vice-President, Mr Speaker, Members of the Senate, and of the House of Representatives.

Yesterday, December 7th, 1941—a date which will live in infamy—the United States of America was suddenly and deliberately attacked by naval and air forces of the Empire of Japan.

The United States was at peace with that nation and, at the solicitation of Japan, was still in conversation with its government and its emperor looking toward the maintenance of peace in the Pacific.

"This form of treachery shall never again endanger us."

Indeed, one hour after Japanese air squadrons had commenced bombing in the American island of Oahu, the Japanese ambassador to the United States and his colleagues delivered to our Secretary of State a formal reply to a recent American message. And while this reply stated that it seemed useless to continue the existing diplomatic negotiations, it contained no threat or hint of war or of armed attack.

It will be recorded that the distance of Hawaii from Japan makes it obvious that the attack was deliberately planned many days or even weeks ago. During the intervening time, the Japanese government has deliberately sought to deceive the United States by false statements and expressions of hope for continued peace.

The attack yesterday on the Hawaiian islands has caused severe damage to American naval and military forces. I regret to tell you that very many American lives have been lost. In addition, American ships have been reported torpedoed on the high seas between San Francisco and Honolulu.

Yesterday, the Japanese government also launched an attack against Malaya.

Last night, Japanese forces attacked Hong Kong.

Last night, Japanese forces attacked Guam.

Last night, Japanese forces attacked the Philippine Islands.

Last night, the Japanese attacked Wake Island.

And this morning, the Japanese attacked Midway Island.

Japan has, therefore, undertaken a surprise offensive extending throughout the Pacific area. The facts of yesterday and today speak for themselves. The people of the United States have already formed their opinions and well understand the implications to the very life and safety of our nation.

As commander in chief of the army and navy, I have directed that all measures be taken for our defense. But always will our whole nation remember the character of the onslaught against us.

No matter how long it may take us to overcome this premeditated invasion, the American people in their righteous might will win through to absolute victory.

I believe that I interpret the will of the Congress and of the people when I assert that we will not only defend ourselves to the uttermost, but will make it very certain that this form of treachery shall never again endanger us.

Hostilities exist. There is no blinking at the fact that our people, our territory, and our interests are in grave danger.

With confidence in our armed forces, with the unbounding determination of our people, we will gain the inevitable triumph—so help us God.

I ask that the Congress declare that since the unprovoked and dastardly attack by Japan on Sunday, December 7th, 1941, a state of war has existed between the United States and the Japanese Empire.

"Form and function seen as one: of such is democracy."

Frank Lloyd Wright

From a lecture given at Princeton (1930) and in London (1939)

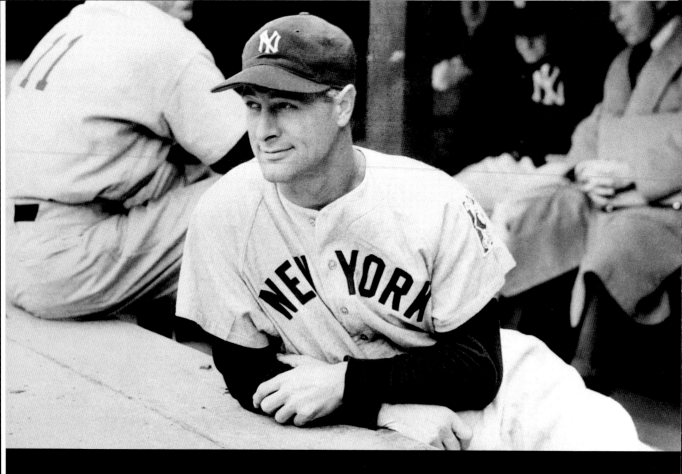

"A bad break."

Lou Gehrig

Farewell to baseball, Lou Gehrig Day, 4 July 1939

Lou Gehrig formed a dream-ticket baseball offensive duo with his team mate Babe Ruth. But despite their symbiotic professional relationship the two men barely spoke to each other off the field. Somewhat overshadowed by the flamboyant Babe, as he was later by Jo DiMaggio, Gehrig was a quiet character—temperamentally well suited to fill the position of Yankees' captain.

The child of German immigrants, Henry Louis Gehrig grew up in a poor neighborhood of New York. At NYC School of Commerce, he was a promising football and baseball player and at 17 was already being compared with Babe Ruth. Gehrig was encouraged to enrol at Columbia University by their athletics manager. But when he was spotted by a Yankee talent scout, his mother's hopes that a university place would lead to a career as an engineer or architect came to nothing.

Gehrig signed to the Yankees in 1923 and left Columbia, where, disadvantaged by his social and financial background, he had never been happy, although he later credited his appreciation of literature and classical music to the time he spent there.

In 1925 Gehrig was substituted for the first baseman Wally Pipp and kept the job. In 1927, 1931, 1934, and 1936 he was named the league's Most Valuable Player. He hit 40 or more home runs in five seasons, including four consecutive home runs in one game alone.

Sturdily built, Gehrig was a left-handed first baseman and one of professional baseball's greatest hitters. One of his most remarkable achievements was his continuity of play, never missing a single game in 14 seasons. He played through injury and illness and later in his career X-rays of his hands showed 17 separate fractures.

Born 19 June 1903 in New York City. Yankees' fans were devastated when Lou Gehrig voluntarily retired from the game in May 1939. Few people knew that he would die within a few years from a paralyzing disease. On 4 July the Yankees held Lou Gehrig Day, at which Gehrig gave this impromptu and touching speech. His words became known as baseball's Gettysburg Address.
Died 2 June 1941 in New York City.

In May 1939 Gehrig's performance began to decline and he decided to step down for the good of the team. At the Mayo Clinic in Rochester he was diagnosed with an incurable degenerative disease, amyotrophic lateral sclerosis, since named Lou Gehrig's Disease.

After his retirement, Gehrig was inducted into baseball's Hall of Fame, without the statutory five-year waiting period. He remained close to the Yankees and on a trip to Cincinnati with them met the major of New York, who asked Gehrig to join the New York City Parole Commission. Although diffident about his abilities, Gehrig was committed to the work, and read up on criminology, sociology, and psychology. In the final year of his life he traveled to Manhattan daily for his new job. "I think that many convicted fellows deserve another chance," he said. "We don't want anyone in jail who can make good."

In 1941, when Gehrig could no longer travel and could barely sign his name, he retired from his parole work. He remained at home, listening to music and opera, and welcoming many visitors. Shortly before his thirty-eighth birthday, he died in his sleep. After his death over 1,500 telegrams and messages flooded into his home, including flowers from President Roosevelt. A former teammate, however, commented, "He doesn't need tributes from anyone. His life and the way he lived were tribute enough."

Fans, for the past two weeks you have been reading about a bad break I got. Yet today I consider myself the luckiest man on the face of the earth.

I have been in ballparks for 17 years and have never received anything but kindness and encouragement from you fans. Look at these grand men. Which of you wouldn't consider it the highlight of his career just to associate with them for even one day?

Sure I'm lucky.

Who wouldn't consider it an honor to have known Jacob Ruppert? Also, the builder of baseball's greatest empire, Ed Barrow? To have spent six years with that wonderful little fellow, Miller Huggins? Then to have spent the next nine years with that outstanding leader, that smart student of psychology, the best manager in baseball today, Joe McCarthy?

Sure I'm lucky.

When the New York Giants, a team you would give your right arm to beat, and vice versa, sends you a gift—that's something. When everybody down to the groundskeepers and those boys in white coats remember you with trophies—that's something.

When you have a father and a mother who work all their lives so you can have an education and build your body—it's a blessing.

When you have a wife who has been a tower of strength and shown more courage than you dreamed existed—that's the finest I know.

So, I close in saying that I might have been given a bad break, but I've got an awful lot to live for.

"I am personally going to shoot that paper-hanging sonofabitch Hitler."

General George S. Patton Jr

Speech to the US Third Army on the eve of D-Day, 5 June, 1944

George Smith Patton Jr was born in 1885 and grew up in an important military family from Virginia. As a child he was keenly interested in the Civil War, especially the great cavalry leaders. Patton graduated from West Point Military Academy in 1909, received a commission in the cavalry and saw tank service in World War I in France, becoming a vigorous advocate of tank warfare. Between the two wars he was active in the formation of tank units and in World War II became a supreme practitioner of mobile armored warfare, playing a key role in the invasion of North Africa in 1942 and the capture of Sicily in 1943, where he commanded the Seventh Army.

The peak of Patton's career came in 1944–5, following the Allied invasion of German-occupied France. When Roosevelt, Churchill and Stalin met at Tehran in 1943, it was agreed that a second front would be opened up on Hitler by an invasion of Western Europe. "Operation Overlord" had been years in the planning, with the accumulation of men and resources in southeast England, the feeding of misinformation to the Germans and air strikes on the French communication systems to disrupt German troop movements. The decision, which rested on the right weather conditions, was made by US General Dwight Eisenhower, Allied Supreme Commander in Europe, that D (for "deliverance") Day would be 6 June 1944.

Born 11 November 1885 in San Gabriel, California.

This plain-speaking speech, given "somewhere in England" on the eve of D-Day in 1944, is typical of George Patton's forthright and frequently profane style. Never using notes, Patton always addressed his men in down-to-earth language, often giving commonsense advice they could follow to avoid being killed or injured. Patton himself said of his swearing, "You can't run an army without profanity; and it has to be eloquent profanity."

Died 21 December 1945 in Germany.

On D-Day a fleet of 5,000 crossed the English Channel carrying British, American, French, and Canadian troops, vehicles and stores and towing artificially constructed harbors ("mulberries") to serve until a French port could be captured. After heavy bombardment by Allied planes and ships, the forces landed on five beaches in Normandy and airborne troops were also dropped. Expecting an assault further north, the Germans were taken by surprise and most beaches were taken swiftly. The first thrust of the invasion was successful, although there were heavy US losses at the beach code-named Omaha.

Patton was given command of the Third Army, which was to be involved in 281 days of combat in France, during which it achieved a spectacular sweep across the country and into Germany. His daring methods brought civilian criticism, largely overlooked by the authorities in acknowledgment of Patton's achievements. However, when Patton himself criticized the Allied post-war denazification policies in Germany in 1945, he was removed from command of the Third Army.

Nicknamed "Old Blood and Guts" by his men, Patton was a colorful, controversial character. He was quick-tempered, tough-minded and outspoken as an officer. He was also a disciplinarian but his own self-sacrifice gained him loyalty from his men. Patton was fatally injured in a car accident in Mannheim in Germany and died in 1945. He is buried among the soldiers who died in the battle of the Bulge in Luxembourg.

You are here today for three reasons. First, because you are here to defend your homes and your loved ones. Second, you are here for your own self-respect, because you would not want to be anywhere else. Third, you are here because you are real men and all real men like to fight. When you, here, every one of you, were kids, you all admired the champion marble player, the fastest runner, the toughest boxer, the big league ball players, and the All-American football players. Americans love a winner. Americans will not tolerate a loser. Americans despise cowards. Americans play to win all of the time. I wouldn't give a hoot in hell for a man who lost and laughed. That's why Americans have never lost nor will ever lose a war; for the very idea of losing is hateful to an American.

You are not all going to die. Only two per cent of you right here today would die in a major battle. Death must not be feared. Death, in time, comes to all men. Yes, every man is scared in his first battle. If he says he's not, he's a liar. Some men are cowards but they fight the same as the brave men or they get the hell slammed out of them watching men fight who are just as scared as they are.

"Americans love a winner."

The real hero is the man who fights even though he is scared. Some men get over their fright in a minute under fire. For some, it takes an hour. For some it takes days. But a real man will never let his fear of death overpower his honor, his sense of duty to his country, and his innate manhood.

Battle is the most magnificent competition in which a human being can indulge. It brings out all that is best and removes all that is base. Americans pride themselves on being he men and they are he men. Remember that the enemy is just as frightened as you are, and probably more so. They are not supermen.

… All of the real heroes are not storybook combat fighters, either. Every single man in this army plays a vital role. Don't ever let up. Don't ever think that your job is unimportant. Every man has a job to do and he must do it. Every man is a vital link in the great chain. What if every truck driver suddenly decided that he didn't like the whine of those shells overhead, turned yellow, and jumped headlong into a ditch? The cowardly bastard could say, "Hell, they won't miss me, just one man in thousands." But, what if every man thought that way? Where in the hell would we be now? What would our country, our loved ones, our homes, even the world, be like? No, goddamnit, Americans don't think like that. Every man does his job. Every man serves the whole. Every department, every unit, is important in the vast scheme of this war.

"The real hero is the man who fights even though he is scared."

… Sure, we want to go home. We want this war over with. The quickest way to get it over with is to go get the bastards who started it. The quicker they are whipped, the quicker we can go home. The shortest way home is through Berlin and Tokyo. And when we get to Berlin, I am personally going to shoot that paper-hanging sonofabitch Hitler. Just like I'd shoot a snake!

… There is one great thing that you men will all be able to say after this war is over and you are home once again. You may be thankful that 20 years from now when you are sitting by the fireplace with your grandson on your knee and he asks you what you did in the great World War II, you won't have to cough, shift him to the other knee and say, "Well, your granddaddy shovelled shit in Louisiana." No, sir, you can look him straight in the eye and say, "Son, your granddaddy rode with the great Third Army and a sonofagoddamnedbitch named Georgie Patton!"

"The reason that we did this job is because it was an organic necessity."

J. Robert Oppenheimer

Los Alamos, New Mexico, 2 November 1945

Physicist J. Robert Oppenheimer directed research at the Manhattan Project, the name given to the team that built and tested the first atomic bomb.

As early as 1939 Albert Einstein and Leo Szilard had outlined the dangers if Nazi laboratories were the first to develop an atomic bomb. Once America had entered the war, President Roosevelt set up a research center and in 1942 Oppenheimer was asked to lead British and American physicists in finding a way to harness nuclear energy for military purposes.

The first atomic bomb was exploded at Alamogordo in New Mexico on 16 July 1945. Some years later, Oppenheimer described his reaction: "We knew the world would not be the same. A few people laughed, a few people cried, most people were silent. I remembered the line from the Hindu scripture, the Bhagavad-Gita ... 'Now, I am become Death, the destroyer of worlds'." President Truman gave orders for a bomb to be used against Japan as soon as possible to bring a swift end to the war. The first bomb was dropped on Hiroshima on 6 August 1945 and a second on Nagasaki three days later. The devastation was far more horrifying than had been anticipated. Japan surrendered on 14 August 1945.

Born 22 April 1904 in New York.
In this extract from a speech given four months after Hiroshima, Oppenheimer explored why scientists created the bomb and considered the future cooperation between nations that would now be necessary. Although he maintained that he felt no guilt for his work on atomic weapons, he never denied his sense of moral responsibility.
Died 18 February 1967 in New York.

Robert Oppenheimer was born in 1904. He studied physics at Harvard and quantum mechanics and relativity at the Cavendish Laboratory at the University of Cambridge, England. From 1929 he held posts at the University of California in Berkeley and the California Institute of Technology, where he established large schools of theoretical physics. A whole generation of physicists owed much to his intelligent and inspiring leadership.

In 1942, as part of the Manhattan Project's research and development work, Oppenheimer was asked to coordinate work on the atomic bomb. He was widely acknowledged as a brilliant director. In October 1945 he resigned and returned to California, although he continued to advise the government on the use and control of nuclear weapons.

Between 1947 and 1952 Oppenheimer was chairman of the board of scientific advisors of the Atomic Energy Commission. In 1949 the board refused to pass a proposal to start the manufacture of hydrogen bombs. This, together with his sharp tongue and views on arms control, made Oppenheimer military and political enemies. His opposition to the hydrogen bomb and alleged contacts with communists led to his being denied security clearance in 1954. However, ten years later the AEC awarded him the prestigious Fermi

Award, recognizing his scientific leadership and groundwork on many peaceful uses of atomic energy. Oppenheimer spent his last years exploring the relationship between science and society. A lifelong cigarette and pipe smoker, he died of throat cancer in 1967.

I should like to talk tonight … as a fellow scientist, and at least as a fellow worrier about the fix we are in.

… In considering what the situation of science is, it may be helpful to think a little of what people said and felt of their motives in coming into this job.

… There was in the first place the great concern that our enemy might develop these weapons before we did, and the feeling—at least, in the early days, the very strong feeling—that without atomic weapons it might be very difficult, it might be an impossible, it might be an incredibly long thing to win the war. These things wore off a little as it became clear that the war would be won in any case. Some people, I think, were motivated by curiosity, and rightly so; and some by a sense of adventure, and rightly so. Others had more political arguments and said, "Well, we know that atomic weapons are in principle possible, and it is not right that the threat of their unrealized possibility should hang over the world. It is right that the world should know what can be done in their field and deal with it."

… And there was finally, and I think rightly, the feeling that there was probably no place in the world where the development of atomic weapons would have a better chance of leading to a reasonable solution, and a smaller chance of leading to disaster, than within the United States. I believe all these things that people said are true, and I think I said them all myself at one time or another. But when you come right down to it the reason that we did this job is because it was an organic necessity.

… If you are a scientist you believe that it is good to find out how the world works; that it is good to find out what the realities are; that it is good to turn over to mankind at large the greatest possible power to control the world and to deal with it according to its lights and its values.

… It is not possible to be a scientist unless you believe that it is good to learn. It is not good to be a scientist, and it is not possible, unless you think that it is of the highest value to share your knowledge, to share it with anyone who is interested. It is not possible to be a scientist unless you believe that the knowledge of the world, and the power which this gives, is a thing which is of

Following World War II the destabilization of Greece had led to civil war and Turkey was also highly unstable. President Harry S. Truman asked Congress for $400 million in military and economic aid for the two countries, insisting that without US aid, the rise of communism in the whole region was inevitable. This aid was granted by law in May 1947, and established the foreign policy that became known as the Truman Doctrine: America would provide money, equipment or military support for any country threatened by communism.

It was the Truman Doctrine that ultimately led to involvement in the Vietnam War, as Truman supplied French forces protecting France's Vietnamese colonies with equipment and military advice to help them fight the communist Ho Chi Minh.

Truman had proved himself a brave commander as a lieutenant in World War I and as a Senator he was known for his diligence, friendliness, and efficiency. He was a popular choice as Vice-President in the 1944 election campaign but when he became President only 82 days later, he was daunted, telling reporters that he felt "like the moon, the stars, and all the planets had fallen on me." Nevertheless, he proved to be more than equal to the role and won a second term in office in 1948. Always ready to take responsibility for the power he carried, he famously kept a plaque on his desk stating "The buck stops here."

Born 8 May 1884, in Lamar, Missouri. Inheriting office on Franklin D. Roosevelt's sudden death, President Harry S. Truman surprised many with his ability to act decisively in difficult times. In the early years of the Cold War he took a firm stand on Soviet expansionist policies in Europe, and stated in his "Truman Doctrine" that the US would fight communist aggression everywhere it occurred. The speech puts the case for aid to specific countries within the broader context of US support for free peoples, and intervention to stem the global communist threat.
Died 26 December 1972, in Kansas City, Missouri.

Soon after he became President, Truman was faced with one of the most controversial decisions ever taken by a US President. In August 1945, he authorized the dropping of the atomic bombs that led to Japanese surrender and the end of World War II. He then instigated a strategy for post-war recovery in Europe, the Marshall Plan, and oversaw the massive airlift of supplies during the blockade of West Berlin in 1948. In 1949 he established the North Atlantic Treaty Organization (NATO). During the Korean War in the 1950s, Truman showed himself unafraid to take a firm stance with the popular but insubordinate General MacArthur. In 1953 he announced the development of the hydrogen bomb.

In domestic policy Truman proposed the Fair Deal, tackling social issues. He also established the desegregation of the military and appointed African-Americans to high-level administrative positions.

Truman declined to run for re-election in 1952, although he was eligible to do so. In the three decades since his death in 1972 he has come to be regarded as one of the greatest twentieth-century Presidents.

The United States has received from the Greek government an urgent appeal for financial and economic assistance. Preliminary reports from the American Economic Mission now in Greece and reports from the American Ambassador in Greece corroborate the statement of the Greek government that assistance is imperative if Greece is to survive as a free nation.

I do not believe that the American people and the Congress wish to turn a deaf ear to the appeal of the Greek government.

… The very existence of the Greek state is today threatened by the terrorist activities of several thousand armed men, led by communists, who defy the government's authority at a number of points, particularly along the northern boundaries. A commission appointed by the United Nations Security Council is at present investigating disturbed conditions in northern Greece and alleged border violations along the frontier between Greece on the one hand and Albania, Bulgaria, and Yugoslavia on the other.

"We must assist free peoples to work out their own destinies in their own way."

Meanwhile, the Greek government is unable to cope with the situation. The Greek army is small and poorly equipped. It needs supplies and equipment if it is to restore authority to the government throughout Greek territory.

Greece must have assistance if it is to become a self-supporting and self-respecting democracy.

The United States must supply this assistance. We have already extended to Greece certain types of relief and economic aid but these are inadequate.

There is no other country to which democratic Greece can turn.

... The Greek government has been operating in an atmosphere of chaos and extremism. It has made mistakes. The extension of aid by this country does not mean that the United States condones everything that the Greek government has done or will do. We have condemned in the past, and we condemn now, extremist measures of the right or the left. We have in the past advised tolerance, and we advise tolerance now. Greece's neighbor, Turkey, also deserves our attention.

... One of the primary objectives of the foreign policy of the United States is the creation of conditions in which we and other nations will be able to work out a way of life free from coercion. This was a fundamental issue in the war with Germany and Japan. Our victory was won over countries which sought to impose their will, and their way of life, upon other nations.

"The free peoples of the world look to us for support in maintaining their freedoms."

... I believe that it must be the policy of the United States to support free peoples who are resisting attempted subjugation by armed minorities or by outside pressures.

I believe that we must assist free peoples to work out their own destinies in their own way.

I believe that our help should be primarily through economic and financial aid which is essential to economic stability and orderly political processes.

The world is not static, and the status quo is not sacred. But we cannot allow changes in the status quo in violation of the Charter of the United Nations by such methods as coercion, or by such subterfuges as political infiltration. In helping free and independent nations to maintain their freedom, the United States will be giving effect to the principles of the Charter of the United Nations.

It is necessary only to glance at a map to realize that the survival and integrity of the Greek nation are of grave importance in a much wider situation. If Greece should fall under the control of an armed minority, the effect upon its neighbor, Turkey, would be immediate and serious. Confusion and disorder might well spread throughout the entire Middle East.

… It would be an unspeakable tragedy if these countries, which have struggled so long against overwhelming odds, should lose that victory for which they sacrificed so much. Collapse of free institutions and loss of independence would be disastrous not only for them but for the world. Discouragement and possibly failure would quickly be the lot of neighboring peoples striving to maintain their freedom and independence.

Should we fail to aid Greece and Turkey in this fateful hour, the effect will be far reaching to the West as well as to the East.

We must take immediate and resolute action.

I therefore ask the Congress to provide authority for assistance to Greece and Turkey in the amount of $400 million for the period ending June 30, 1948.

… In addition to funds, I ask the Congress to authorize the detail of American civilian and military personnel to Greece and Turkey, at the request of those countries, to assist in the tasks of reconstruction, and for the purpose of supervising the use of such financial and material assistance as may be furnished. I recommend that authority also be provided for the instruction and training of selected Greek and Turkish personnel.

… This is a serious course upon which we embark. I would not recommend it except that the alternative is much more serious.

The United States contributed $341 billion toward winning World War II. This is an investment in world freedom and world peace. The assistance that I am recommending for Greece and Turkey amounts to little more than one tenth of one percent of this investment. It is only common sense that we should safeguard this investment and make sure that it was not in vain.

The seeds of totalitarian regimes are nurtured by misery and want. They spread and grow in the evil soil of poverty and strife. They reach their full growth when the hope of a people for a better life has died. We must keep that hope alive. The free peoples of the world look to us for support in maintaining their freedoms. If we falter in our leadership, we may endanger the peace of the world, and we shall surely endanger the welfare of this nation.

Great responsibilities have been placed upon us by the swift movement of events. I am confident that the Congress will face these responsibilities squarely.

"The international Magna Carta of all men everywhere."

Eleanor Roosevelt

Approving the Universal Declaration of Human Rights, Paris, France, 9 December 1948

Anna Eleanor Roosevelt was orphaned as a child and raised by her maternal grandmother, a distant and emotionally cold woman. Despite being the favorite niece of President Teddy Roosevelt, she suffered from constant self-doubt and depression. This was not helped by the jealousy within her family after her marriage in 1905 to her handsome cousin, Franklin, or by life with her domineering mother-in-law.

The Roosevelts had six children, one of whom died in infancy, and for many years Eleanor's horizons were bounded by domesticity and motherhood. Then in 1918, she discovered that her husband was having an affair with Lucy Mercer, her social secretary, and as she later wrote: "The bottom dropped out of my own particular world. I faced myself, my surroundings, my world, honestly for the first time." The couple did not divorce but the discovery strengthened Eleanor's independence. She began to help her husband in his political career and when he was paralyzed by polio in 1921 she became his "eyes and ears," traveling the country on his behalf. Eleanor later supported Franklin's bids for the vice-presidency and presidency, which he first won in 1932. However, by this time they were leading virtually separate lives.

Eleanor became an acknowledged figure in her own right, with an independent agenda. A contemporary political worker

Born 11 October 1884 in New York City. As a shy and insecure young woman, Eleanor Roosevelt would never have believed herself capable of making this speech. She blossomed into one of the twentieth century's greatest public figures. In 1948, Eleanor was Chair of the United Nations Commission on Human Rights. She gave this speech, championing the Universal Declaration of Human Rights, in Paris on 9 December. Later that night, the Declaration was unanimously adopted by the UN General Assembly.
Died 7 November 1962 in New York City.

recalled, "One saw her as a dominant guide, colleague and co-worker of the President, not just as his wife." An area that she made uniquely her own, and at which she was sometimes at odds with her husband, was civil rights. She lobbied him to tackle discrimination in the administration of his New Deal projects.

In 1932 her lifelong friend, reporter Lorena Hickok, suggested that the new First Lady should write a daily newspaper column, which Eleanor began in 1935. It continued uninterrupted—apart from four days in 1945 when Franklin Roosevelt died—for six days a week, until 1962.

After Franklin's funeral in April 1945, Eleanor told reporters, "The story is over," but this was far from true. Within a year of his death Eleanor was working as a US spokesperson at the United Nations. She also became a significant force in Democratic politics, overcoming her long-held dislike of the Kennedy family to support John F. Kennedy's presidential campaign in 1960. Described by President Harry S. Truman as "the First Lady of the world," embassy flags flew at half-mast the world over the day after her death in 1962.

The long and meticulous study and debate of which this Universal Declaration of Human Rights is the product means that it reflects the composite views of the many men and governments who have contributed to its formulation. Not every man nor every government can have what he wants in a document of this kind. There are of course particular provisions in the declaration before us with which we are not fully satisfied. I have no doubt this is true of other delegations, and it would still be true if we continued our labors over many years. Taken as a whole the Delegation of the United States believes that this is a good document—even a great document—and we propose to give it our full support. The position of the United States on the various parts of the declaration is a matter of record in the Third Committee. I shall not burden the Assembly, and particularly my colleagues of the Third Committee, with a restatement of that position here.

… In giving our approval to the declaration today it is of primary importance that we keep clearly in mind the basic character of the document. It is not a treaty; it is not an international agreement. It is not and does not purport to be a statement of basic principles of law or legal obligation. It is a declaration of basic principles of human rights and freedoms, to be stamped with the approval of the General Assembly by formal vote of its members, and to serve as a common standard of achievement for all peoples of all nations.

"It is a declaration of basic principles of human rights and freedom."

We stand today at the threshold of a great event both in the life of the United Nations and in the life of mankind, that is the approval by the General Assembly of the Universal Declaration of Human Rights recommended by the Third Committee. This declaration may well become the international Magna Carta of all men everywhere. We hope its proclamation by the General Assembly will be an event comparable to the proclamation of the Declaration of the Rights of Man by the French people in 1789, the adoption of the Bill of Rights by the people of the United States, and the adoption of comparable declarations at different times in other countries.

At a time when there are so many issues on which we find it difficult to reach a common basis of agreement, it is a significant fact that 58 states have found such a large measure of agreement in the complex field of human rights. This must be taken as testimony of our common aspiration first voiced in the Charter of the United Nations to lift men everywhere to a higher standard of life and to a greater enjoyment of freedom. Man's desire for peace lies behind this declaration. The realization that the flagrant violation of human rights by Nazi and Fascist countries sowed the seeds of the last world war has supplied the impetus for the work which brings us to the moment of achievement here today.

"This declaration may well become the international Magna Carta of all men everywhere."

… This declaration is based upon the spiritual fact that man must have freedom in which to develop his full stature and through common effort to raise the level of human dignity. We have much to do to fully achieve and to assure the rights set forth in this declaration. But having them put before us with the moral backing of 58 nations will be a great step forward.

"Man's desire for peace lies behind this declaration."

As we here bring to fruition our labors on this Declaration of Human Rights, we must at the same time rededicate ourselves to the unfinished task which lies before us. We can now move on with new courage and inspiration to the completion of an international covenant on human rights and of measures for the implementation of human rights.

"Enemies from within."

Joseph R. McCarthy
Speech to the Republican Women's Club of Wheeling, West Virginia,
9 February 1950

The fifth child of devout Catholic parents, Joseph McCarthy was a shy and unpopular child, over-protected by his mother. After initially training as an engineer, he turned to law, graduating in 1935. Resourceful, energetic, stubborn, and aggressive, in 1939 he became a state circuit judge, the youngest in Wisconsin's history. However, his legal career was tainted by early doubts about his probity. In 1942 he served in the Marine Corps in the South Pacific.

In 1946, McCarthy became Senator for Wisconsin, having made false and highly injurious claims against the Republican incumbent. His early senatorial career was undistinguished, marked by minor scandals and squabbles with other Senators, often over proposals that benefited his own business interests. Then in January 1950 he began to focus on communist infiltration of the government, a growing public concern.

McCarthy's speech in early 1950 brought him far greater media attention than he anticipated. In the following days he kept changing the numbers of "known communists" he could identify. Later, while testifying before the Senate Committee on Foreign Relations, he was unable to produce the name of any card-carrying members of the Communist Party in any government department. Nonetheless, his rise to power became inexorable as he exploited the national *zeitgeist* of fear about the spread of communism.

Born 14 November 1908 in Grand Chute, Wisconsin.

With this speech Senator Joseph McCarthy launched his reign of terror against prominent public figures, naming those he believed were communist sympathizers. His accusation brought McCarthy unprecedented power in the Republican Party until 1954, when he finally overreached himself. This short period of history led to McCarthy's name becoming a synonym for the use of smear tactics to destroy someone's political and personal reputation. Died 2 May 1957 in Bethesda, Maryland.

McCarthy's personal agenda in the campaign was apparent. He destroyed the reputations and careers of many of his opponents, including Millard Tydings, chair of the committee that had found his initial claims groundless. His own colleagues were torn between their fear of him and his usefulness in harrying the Truman administration, especially Secretary of State Dean Acheson.

In 1952, following the Republicans' electoral triumph, McCarthy was appointed chair of the Senate Permanent Subcommittee on Investigations. For the next two years he continued to make accusations about communist influence in public life. Not even President Eisenhower was exempt. Although he loathed McCarthy and wanted his removal, Eisenhower was hampered by general approval of the Senator's campaign.

Eventually, however, McCarthy grew reckless and in a key error of judgment attempted to reveal a spy ring in the Army Signal Corps. His hectoring cross-examination, damaging innuendo, and personal disrespect for individuals were publicly displayed in televised hearings in 1954, and as a result McCarthy lost support. He was replaced as chairman of the investigating committee, and in December 1954 Senate proposed a vote of censure for "conduct contrary to Senate traditions." McCarthy's political career sank into oblivion and he succumbed to alcohol-related illness that finally killed him in 1957.

Tonight as we celebrate the one hundred and forty-first birthday of one of the greatest men in American history, I would like to be able to talk about what a glorious day today is in the history of the world. As we celebrate the birth of this man, who with his whole heart and soul hated war, I would like to be able to speak of peace in our time, of war being outlawed, and of worldwide disarmament. These would be truly appropriate things to be able to mention as we celebrate the birthday of Abraham Lincoln.

Five years after a world war has been won, men's hearts should anticipate a long peace, and men's minds should be free from the heavy weight that comes with war. But this is not such a period, for this is not a period of peace. This is a time of the "cold war." This is a time when all the world is split into two vast, increasingly hostile armed camps, a time of a great armaments race. Today we can almost physically hear the mutterings and rumblings of an invigorated god of war. You can see it, feel it, and hear it all the way from the hills of Indochina, from the shores of Formosa, right over into the very heart of Europe itself.

… Today we are engaged in a final, all-out battle between communistic atheism and Christianity. The modern champions of communism have selected this as the time. And, ladies and gentlemen, the chips are down; they are truly down.

… Six years ago, at the time of the first conference to map out the peace—Dumbarton Oaks—there was within the Soviet orbit 180 million people. Lined up on the anti-totalitarian side there were in the world at that time roughly 1,625,000,000 people. Today, only six years later, there are 800 million people under the absolute domination of Soviet Russia, an increase of over 400 percent. On our side, the figure has shrunk to around 500 million. In other words, in less than six years the odds have changed from 9–1 in our favor to 8–3 against us. This indicates the swiftness of the tempo of communist victories and American defeats in the cold war. As one of our outstanding historical figures once said, "When a great democracy is destroyed, it will not be because of enemies from without but rather because of enemies from within." The truth of this statement is becoming terrifyingly clear as we see this country each day losing on every front.

… The reason why we find ourselves in a position of impotency is not because our only powerful, potential enemy has sent men to invade our shores, but rather because of the traitorous actions of those who have been treated so well by this nation. It has not been the less fortunate or members of minority groups who have been selling this nation out, but rather those who have had all the benefits that the wealthiest nation on earth has had to offer: the finest homes, the finest college education, and the finest jobs in government we can give.

"When a great democracy is destroyed it will not be from enemies from without but rather because of enemies from within."

This is glaringly true in the State Department. There the bright young men who are born with silver spoons in their mouths are the ones who have been worst.

… I have in my hand 57 cases of individuals who would appear to be either card-carrying members or certainly loyal to the Communist Party, but who nevertheless are still helping to shape our foreign policy.

… As you know, very recently the Secretary of State proclaimed his loyalty to a man guilty of what has always been considered as the most abominable of all crimes—of being a traitor to the people who gave him a position of great trust. The Secretary of State, in attempting to justify his continued devotion to the man who sold out the Christian world to the atheistic world, referred to Christ's Sermon on the Mount as a justification and reason therefore, and the reaction of the American people to this would have made the heart of Abraham Lincoln happy. When this pompous diplomat in striped pants, with a phony British accent, proclaimed to the American people that Christ on the Mount endorsed communism, high treason, and betrayal of a sacred trust, the blasphemy was so great that it awakened the dormant indignation of the American people.

He has lighted the spark which is resulting in a moral uprising and will end only when the whole sorry mess of twisted, warped thinkers are swept from the national scene so that we may have a new birth of national honor and decency in government.

"Ask not what your country can do for you; ask what you can do for your country."

John F. Kennedy
Inaugural address, Washington, 20 January 1961

"Ich bin ein Berliner."
West Berlin, Germany, 26 June 1963

"Watchmen on the walls of world freedom."
Undelivered speech, Dallas, Texas, 22 November 1963

Widely admired both at home and abroad, John F. Kennedy was the first Roman Catholic and, at 43, the youngest man to be elected President. The eloquent speech he gave at his inauguration swept away many people's fears that he was too young and inexperienced for the job.

Kennedy's arrival in the White House on 20 January 1961 followed a narrow electoral victory over the Republican Richard Nixon, who had been Vice-President for eight years. Kennedy promised tough defense policies but progressive health, housing, and civil rights programs, and promoted his "New Frontier" campaign to bring the nation out of economic slump. Many innovative features of his campaign became established elements of future campaigns, including televised debates with his opponent. In these, Kennedy appeared personable and relaxed, while Nixon looked tense and uneasy. Kennedy stressed the need for change to stop America's decline as a world power, which he claimed was the result of Eisenhower's presidency.

Once in office, Kennedy appointed a cabinet of young able men, including some Republicans selected for their talent. He also appointed his brother Robert, his closest friend and ally, as Attorney General even though he was only 35. Together with his wife, Jacqueline, Kennedy revitalized the White House, encouraging intellectual and artistic activity.

Born 29 May 1917 in Boston, Massachusetts. President John F. Kennedy was a World War II hero and Pulitzer Prize winner (for his biography *Profiles in Courage*, 1957). An admirer of fine oratory, he refined and edited his inaugural address for two months before it was given. *"Ich bin ein Berliner,"* given to an audience of Germans on either side of the newly erected Berlin Wall, is credited as marking a turning point in the Cold War. Kennedy was killed on the day he was due to give the final speech included here, a reflective address to educational and political leaders in Dallas during his re-election campaign.
Assassinated 22 November 1963 in Dallas, Texas.

It is hard to assess Kennedy's place in history because only 34 months after he became President he was shot dead in Dallas during his campaign for re-election. By then he had achieved political stature through his handling of the Cuban Missile Crisis in October 1962 and the signing of the nuclear test ban treaty with Russia in 1963. The American economy was greatly improved, civil rights laws were on the statute books and the space program, with Kennedy's mandate to put an American on the moon before the end of the decade, had begun. However, American involvement in Vietnam was becoming a major issue, and Kennedy referred to it as "the worst problem we've got."

rightly alarmed by the steady spread of the deadly atom, yet both racing to alter that uncertain balance of terror that stays the hand of mankind's final war. So let us begin anew—remembering on both sides that civility is not a sign of weakness, and sincerity is always subject to proof.

"This hemisphere intends to remain the master of its own house."

Let us never negotiate out of fear. But let us never fear to negotiate.

Let both sides explore what problems unite us instead of belaboring those problems which divide us.

Let both sides, for the first time, formulate serious and precise proposals for the inspection and control of arms, and bring the absolute power to destroy other nations under the absolute control of all nations.

Let both sides seek to invoke the wonders of science instead of its terrors. Together let us explore the stars, conquer the deserts, eradicate disease, tap the ocean depths, and encourage the arts and commerce.

Let both sides unite to heed, in all corners of the earth, the command of Isaiah: to "undo the heavy burdens ... and let the oppressed go free."

And if a beachhead of cooperation may push back the jungle of suspicion, let both sides join in creating a new endeavor—not a new balance of power, but a new world of law—where the strong are just, and the weak secure, and the peace preserved.

All this will not be finished in the first one hundred days. Nor will it be finished in the first one thousand days; nor in the life of this Administration; nor even perhaps in our lifetime on this planet. But let us begin.

In your hands, my fellow citizens, more than mine, will rest the final success or failure of our course. Since this country was founded, each generation of Americans has been summoned to give testimony to its national loyalty. The graves of young Americans who answered the call to service surround the globe.

Now the trumpet summons us again—not as a call to bear arms, though arms we need; not as a call to battle, though embattled we are—but a call to bear the burden of a long twilight struggle, year in and year out, rejoicing in hope, patient in tribulation, a struggle against the common enemies of man: tyranny, poverty, disease, and war itself.

Can we forge against these enemies a grand and global alliance, North and South, East and West, that can assure a more fruitful life for all mankind? Will you join in that historic effort?

In the long history of the world, only a few generations have been granted the role of defending freedom in its hour of maximum danger. I do not shrink from this responsibility. I welcome it. I do not believe that any of us would exchange places with any other people or any other generation. The energy, the faith, the devotion which we bring to this endeavor will light our country and all who serve it. And the glow from that fire can truly light the world.

"Let us never negotiate out of fear. But let us never fear to negotiate."

And so, my fellow Americans, ask not what your country can do for you; ask what you can do for your country.

My fellow citizens of the world, ask not what America will do for you, but what together we can do for the freedom of man.

Finally, whether you are citizens of America or citizens of the world, ask of us here the same high standards of strength and sacrifice which we ask of you. With a good conscience our only sure reward, with history the final judge of our deeds, let us go forth to lead the land we love, asking His blessing and His help, but knowing that here on earth God's work must truly be our own.

When the Russians built the Berlin Wall in August 1961 to stem the flow of emigrants from East Berlin, Kennedy rejected advice to smash it down through force. On visiting West Berlin in 1963 he delivered a rousing speech in which he cited the wall as the "most obvious and vivid demonstration of the failure of the communist system" and "an offense against humanity." West Berliners loved the speech and Kennedy is widely remembered for it, but the problem of the wall remained for another 26 years.

I am proud to come to this city as the guest of your distinguished Mayor, who has symbolized throughout the world the fighting spirit of West Berlin. And I am proud to visit the Federal Republic with your distinguished Chancellor who for so many years has committed Germany to democracy and freedom and progress, and to come here in the company of my fellow American, General Clay, who has been in this city during its great moments of crisis and will come again if ever needed.

Two thousand years ago, the proudest boast was *civis Romanus sum*. Today, in the world of freedom, the proudest boast is *Ich bin ein Berliner*.

I appreciate my interpreter translating my German.

"Freedom is indivisible, and when one man is enslaved, all are not free."

There are many people in the world who really don't understand, or say they don't, what is the great issue between the free world and the communist world.

Let them come to Berlin.

There are some who say that communism is the wave of the future.

Let them come to Berlin.

And there are some who say, in Europe and elsewhere, we can work with the communists.

Let them come to Berlin.

And there are even a few who say that it is true that communism is an evil system, but it permits us to make economic progress.

Lass' sie nach Berlin kommen. Let them come to Berlin.

Freedom has many difficulties and democracy is not perfect. But we have never had to put a wall up to keep our people in—to prevent them from leaving us. I want to say on behalf of my countrymen who live many miles away on the other side of the Atlantic, who are far distant from you, that they take the greatest pride, that they have been able to share with you, even from a distance, the story of the last 18 years. I know of no town, no city, that has been besieged for 18 years that still lives with the vitality and the force, and the hope, and the determination of the city of West Berlin.

While the wall is the most obvious and vivid demonstration of the failures of the communist system—for all the world to see—we take no satisfaction in it; for it is, as your Mayor has said, an offense not only against history but an offense against humanity, separating families, dividing husbands and wives and brothers and sisters, and dividing a people who wish to be joined together.

What is true of this city is true of Germany: real, lasting peace in Europe can never be assured as long as one German out of four is denied the elementary right of free men, and that is to make a free choice. In 18 years of peace and good faith, this generation of Germans has earned the right to be free, including the right to unite their families and their nation in lasting peace, with good will to all people.

You live in a defended island of freedom, but your life is part of the main. So let me ask you, as I close, to lift your eyes beyond the dangers of today, to the hopes of tomorrow, beyond the freedom merely of this city of Berlin, or your country of Germany, to the advance of freedom everywhere, beyond the wall to the day of peace with justice, beyond yourselves and ourselves to all mankind.

"All free men, wherever they may live, are citizens of Berlin."

Freedom is indivisible, and when one man is enslaved, all are not free. When all are free, then we can look forward to that day when this city will be joined as one and this country and this great Continent of Europe in a peaceful and hopeful globe. When that day finally comes, as it will, the people of West Berlin can take sober satisfaction in the fact that they were in the front lines for almost two decades.

All free men, wherever they may live, are citizens of Berlin.

And, therefore, as a free man, I take pride in the words *Ich bin ein Berliner*.

On 22 November 1963, President Kennedy was due to speak to the Dallas Citizens' Council and members of the Dallas Assembly, at the new Graduate Research Center in the city. His speech was carefully tuned to his audience. It alluded directly to the uses and limitations of the sort of rhetoric for which he himself was so admired, and recalled the achievements and challenges of his first administration. It also evoked the imagery and phrasing of his powerful inauguration address, with its references to a new generation and quotes from scripture. The speech, of course, was never delivered and from that day Dallas would be permanently associated with the tragedy of Kennedy's death.

This link between leadership and learning is not only essential at the community level. It is even more indispensable in world affairs. Ignorance and misinformation can handicap the progress of a city or a company, but they can, if allowed to prevail in foreign policy, handicap this country's security. In a world of complex and continuing problems, in a world full of frustrations and irritations, America's leadership must be guided by the lights of learning and reason or else those who confuse rhetoric with reality and the plausible with the possible will gain the popular ascendancy with their seemingly swift and simple solutions to every world problem.

… The United States is a peaceful nation. And where our strength and determination are clear, our words need merely to convey conviction, not belligerence. If we are strong, our strength will speak for itself. If we are weak, words will be of no help.

I realize that this nation often tends to identify turning-points in world affairs with the major addresses which preceded them. But it was not the Monroe Doctrine that kept all Europe away from this hemisphere—it was the strength of the British fleet and the width of the Atlantic Ocean. It was not General Marshall's speech at Harvard which kept communism out of Western Europe— it was the strength and stability made possible by our military and economic assistance.

"If we are strong, our strength will speak for itself. If we are weak, words will be of no help."

In this administration also it has been necessary at times to issue specific warnings—warnings that we could not stand by and watch the communists conquer Laos by force, or intervene in the Congo, or swallow West Berlin, or maintain offensive missiles on Cuba. But while our goals were at least temporarily obtained in these and other instances, our successful defense of freedom was due not to the words we used, but to the strength we stood ready to use on behalf of the principles we stand ready to defend.

… Finally, it should be clear by now that a nation can be no stronger abroad than she is at home. Only an America which practices what it preaches about equal rights and social justice will be respected by those whose choice affects our future. Only an America which has fully educated its citizens is fully capable of tackling the complex problems and perceiving the hidden dangers of the world in which we live. And only an America which is growing and prospering economically can sustain the worldwide defenses of freedom, while demonstrating to all concerned the opportunities of our system and society.

> "We in this country, in this generation, are—by destiny rather than choice—the watchmen on the walls of world freedom."

… America today is stronger than ever before. Our adversaries have not abandoned their ambitions, our dangers have not diminished, our vigilance cannot be relaxed. But now we have the military, the scientific, and the economic strength to do whatever must be done for the preservation and promotion of freedom.

That strength will never be used in pursuit of aggressive ambitions—it will always be used in pursuit of peace. It will never be used to promote provocations—it will always be used to promote the peaceful settlement of disputes.

We in this country, in this generation, are—by destiny rather than choice—the watchmen on the walls of world freedom. We ask, therefore, that we may be worthy of our power and responsibility, that we may exercise our strength with wisdom and restraint, and that we may achieve in our time and for all time the ancient vision of "peace on earth, good will toward men." That must always be our goal, and the righteousness of our cause must always underlie our strength. For as was written long ago: "Except the Lord keep the city, the watchman waketh but in vain."

"I have a dream."

Martin Luther King Jr

Lincoln Memorial, Washington DC, 28 August 1963

"I've seen the promised land."

Memphis, Tennessee, 3 April 1968

Martin Luther King Jr was born in Atlanta, Georgia to the Reverend and Mrs Martin Luther King. In 1947 he decided to follow his father and become a Baptist minister, delivering his first sermon in his father's church in the summer of that year. The following year he was ordained as a Baptist minister and received his BA degree in sociology from Moorhouse College.

The event that is credited with starting King on his civil rights crusade occurred in 1955. Rosa Parks, a black seamstress traveling home from work in Montgomery, Alabama, took a seat in the rear section of a bus reserved for black passengers. As the bus began to fill, and the forward seats reserved for whites were taken, the driver told her to give up her seat to a white male passenger. When Rosa refused she was arrested. The next day, King arrived in town and launched the Montgomery Bus Boycott. After deliberating for over a year, the Supreme Court ruled that Montgomery's segregation laws were unconstitutional and ordered the integration of the city's buses.

In 1957 King founded the Southern Christian Leadership Conference (SCLC), an association of black churches dedicated to civil rights reform through non-violent civil disobedience, a principle advocated by Mahatma Gandhi, whom King admired. The SCLC organized a series of peaceful protest marches throughout the US.

Born 15 January 1929 in Atlanta, Georgia. Martin Luther King Jr was a major figure in the civil rights movement, winning the Nobel Peace Prize for his work in 1964. His speech "I have a dream," a vision of an America rid of racial tension, has been voted the finest speech in American history. King gave his final speech, "I've seen the promised land," the night before his death and it has since assumed a poignantly prophetic quality.
Assassinated 4 April 1968 in Memphis, Tennessee.
Martin Luther King Day is observed every year on the third Monday in January.

King's most famous speech "I have a dream," was delivered to 250,000 civil rights supporters on the steps of the Lincoln Memorial in Washington, at the culmination of the March on Washington for Jobs and Freedom, in August 1963. The speech is credited with mobilizing supporters of desegregation and prompting the 1964 Civil Rights Act.

The biggest crowd ever assembled in Washington heard King speak. The march had been a success and there was a general feeling that something momentous had been achieved. Whether King had a sense that he was creating his place in history is something that later commentators would speculate about. What is clear is that his speech was timely, adding exactly the right note to the civil rights debate at the right time. Sadly, his blend of moral indignation and Christian values was soon to cost him his life.

go back to South Carolina, go back to Georgia, go back to Louisiana, go back to the slums and ghettos of our northern cities, knowing that somehow this situation can and will be changed. Let us not wallow in the valley of despair, I say to you today, my friends. And so even though we face the difficulties of today and tomorrow, I still have a dream. It is a dream deeply rooted in the American dream.

I have a dream that one day this nation will rise up and live out the true meaning of its creed: We hold these truths to be self-evident that all men are created equal.

"I have a dream today!"

I have a dream that one day on the red hills of Georgia the sons of former slaves and the sons of former slave owners will be able to sit down together at the table of brotherhood.

I have a dream that one day even the state of Mississippi, a state sweltering with the heat of injustice, sweltering with the heat of oppression, will be transformed into an oasis of freedom and justice.

I have a dream that my four little children will one day live in a nation where they will not be judged by the color of their skin but by the content of their character. I have a dream today!

I have a dream that one day, down in Alabama, with its vicious racists, with its governor having his lips dripping with the words of interposition and nullification; one day right down in Alabama little black boys and black girls will be able to join hands with little white boys and white girls as sisters and brothers. I have a dream today!

I have a dream that one day every valley shall be exalted, and every hill and mountain shall be made low, the rough places will be made plain, and the crooked places will be made straight, and the glory of the Lord shall be revealed and all flesh shall see it together.

This is our hope. This is the faith that I will go back to the South with. With this faith we will be able to hew out of the mountain of despair a stone of hope. With this faith we will be able to transform the jangling discords of our nation into a beautiful symphony of brotherhood. With this faith we will be able to work together, to pray together, to struggle together, to go to jail together, to stand up for freedom together, knowing that we will be free one day. And this will be the day, this will be the day when all of God's children will be able to sing with new meaning, "My country 'tis of thee, sweet land of liberty, of thee I sing. Land where my fathers died, land of the Pilgrim's pride, from every mountainside, let freedom ring!" And if America is to be a great nation, this must become true.

And so let freedom ring from the prodigious hilltops of New Hampshire.

"From every mountainside, let freedom ring!"

Let freedom ring from the mighty mountains of New York.

Let freedom ring from the heightening Alleghenies of Pennsylvania.

Let freedom ring from the snow-capped Rockies of Colorado.

Let freedom ring from the curvaceous slopes of California.

But not only that. Let freedom ring from Stone Mountain of Georgia.

Let freedom ring from Lookout Mountain of Tennessee.

Let freedom ring from every hill and molehill of Mississippi, from every mountainside, let freedom ring!

And when this happens, when we allow freedom to ring, when we let it ring from every village and every hamlet, from every state and every city, we will be able to speed up that day when all of God's children, black men and white men, Jews and Gentiles, Protestants and Catholics, will be able to join hands and sing in the words of the old Negro spiritual, "Free at last, free at last. Thank God Almighty, we are free at last."

Four years later, on 4 April 1968, Martin Luther King Jr was killed by a sniper's bullet while standing on the balcony of the Lorraine Motel in Memphis, Tennessee, where he was to lead a protest march in sympathy with striking garbage workers in the city. The day before, he had given a speech in which he recalled an earlier assassination attempt and mentioned threats that he had recently received. His prophetic speech ended on a note of serenity: "I'm happy, tonight. I'm not worried about anything. I'm not fearing any man."

You know, several years ago, I was in New York City autographing the first book that I had written. And while sitting there autographing books, a demented black woman came up. The only question I heard from her was, "Are you Martin Luther King?"

And I was looking down writing, and I said yes. And the next minute I felt something beating on my chest. Before I knew it I had been stabbed by this demented woman. I was rushed to Harlem Hospital. It was a dark Saturday afternoon. And that blade had gone through, and the X-rays revealed that the tip of the blade was on the edge of my aorta, the main artery. And once that's punctured, you drown in your own blood—that's the end of you.

It came out in the *New York Times* the next morning, that if I had sneezed, I would have died. Well, about four days later, they allowed me, after the operation, after my chest had been opened, and the blade had been taken out, to move around in the wheel chair in the hospital. They allowed me to read some of the mail that came in, and from all over the states, and the world, kind letters came in. I read a few, but one of them I will never forget. I had received one from the President and the Vice-President. I've forgotten what those telegrams said. I'd received a visit and a letter from the Governor of New York, but I've forgotten what the letter said. But there was another letter that came from a little girl, a young girl who was a student at the White Plains High School. And I looked at that letter, and I'll never forget it. It said simply, "Dear Dr King: I am a ninth-grade student at the White Plains High School." She said, "While it should not matter, I would like to mention that I am a white girl. I read in the paper of your misfortune, and of your suffering. And I read that if you had sneezed, you would have died. And I'm simply writing you to say that I'm so happy that you didn't sneeze."

"Whenever men and women straighten their backs up, they are going somewhere, because a man can't ride your back unless it is bent."

And I want to say tonight, I want to say that I am happy that I didn't sneeze. Because if I had sneezed, I wouldn't have been around here in 1960, when students all over the South started sitting in at lunch counters. And I knew that as they were sitting in, they were really standing up for the best in the American dream. And taking the whole nation back to those great wells of democracy which were dug deep by the Founding Fathers in the Declaration of Independence and the Constitution. If I had sneezed, I wouldn't have been around in 1962, when Negroes in Albany, Georgia, decided to straighten their backs up. And whenever men and women straighten their backs up, they are going somewhere, because a man can't ride your back unless it is bent. If I had sneezed, I wouldn't have been here in 1963, when the black people of Birmingham, Alabama, aroused the conscience of this nation, and brought into being the Civil Rights Bill. If I had sneezed, I wouldn't have had a chance later that year, in August, to try to tell America about a dream that I had had. If I had sneezed, I wouldn't have been down in Selma, Alabama, to see the great movement there. If I had sneezed, I wouldn't have been in Memphis to see a community rally around those brothers and sisters who are suffering. I'm so happy that I didn't sneeze.

"I've been to the mountaintop. ...And I've seen the promised land."

And they were telling me, now it doesn't matter now. It really doesn't matter what happens now. I left Atlanta this morning, and as we got started on the plane, there were six of us, the pilot said over the public address system, "We are sorry for the delay, but we have Dr Martin Luther King on the plane. And to be sure that all of the bags were checked, and to be sure that nothing would be wrong with the plane, we had to check out everything carefully. And we've had the plane protected and guarded all night."

And then I got into Memphis. And some began to say the threats, or talk about the threats that were out. What would happen to me from some of our sick white brothers?

Well, I don't know what will happen now. We've got some difficult days ahead. But it doesn't matter with me now. Because I've been to the mountaintop. And I don't mind. Like anybody, I would like to live a long life. Longevity has its place. But I'm not concerned about that now. I just want to do God's will. And He's allowed me to go up to the mountain. And I've looked over. And I've seen the promised land. I may not get there with you. But I want you to know tonight, that we, as a people will get to the promised land. And I'm happy, tonight. I'm not worried about anything. I'm not fearing any man. Mine eyes have seen the glory of the coming of the Lord.

"And we shall overcome."

Lyndon B. Johnson

Address to a Joint Session of Congress, 15 March 1965

Lyndon Baines Johnson grew up in a poor Texan farming community and trained as a teacher before entering politics. He was profoundly affected by the social and educational deprivation he witnessed when teaching Mexican immigrants and his first public position was as an official of the National Youth Administration.

At this time (1935–7) Johnson caught Franklin Roosevelt's eye and became one of his protégés. He ran successfully for the House of Representatives and represented his district in the House for nearly 12 years, with only a brief interruption for active duty in World War II.

In 1948 Johnson won a seat in the Senate. It was the start of a long career, in which he became whip in 1951, minority leader in 1953, and, aged 46, the youngest ever majority leader. In 1956 he was the obvious choice for the Democratic nomination for President, a position he worked extremely hard for by ensuring the passage of highly progressive social legislation. However, Johnson unexpectedly lost the nomination to the younger and far less experienced John Kennedy. To the surprise of many, he accepted Kennedy's invitation to be Vice-President. Managing his disappointment, Johnson campaigned wholeheartedly for Kennedy and many felt that his ties with the southern States were a key factor in Kennedy's victory.

Born 27 August 1908 in Gillespie County, Texas. Despite the passing of the Civil Rights Act in 1964, blacks in the South were still unable to vote freely. In 1965 state troopers disrupted a peaceful protest march led by Martin Luther King Jr in Selma, Alabama. During the violence that followed, a white Unitarian Minister was killed. President Lyndon B. Johnson's powers of oratory and personal commitment to civil rights are well illustrated in the speech he gave after the violence, when he borrowed the civil rights slogan, "We shall overcome." Died 22 January 1973 in Johnson City, Texas.

Once elected Kennedy relied on his brother Robert as his closest adviser, leaving Johnson idle and unable to apply his deep political experience. However, when Johnson became President on the assassination of Kennedy in November 1963, he acted swiftly to calm national hysteria and subsequently worked hard to get Kennedy's unachieved legislative agenda enacted.

LBJ (as he was popularly known) committed vast sums to his "Great Society" program, including the introduction of Medicare and Medicaid. After violence in Alabama, the Voting Rights Act was enacted in August 1965, ending the discriminatory use of criteria to limit black votes. But despite Johnson's commitment to civil rights, continuing racial unrest at home, and the Vietnam War, overshadowed his achievements. Johnson feared that losing in Vietnam would lead to defeat for his administration and the loss of his cherished domestic reforms. But the war was a massive drain on money and young lives, and he was vilified for it.

Aware of his unpopularity, Johnson announced his surprise decision not to stand for a second term in a television broadcast in 1967. He then committed himself to working for peace in Vietnam. After years of overwork and poor lifestyle, he died of a heart attack in January 1973, less than a week before a peace agreement on Vietnam was signed in Paris.

Rarely in any time does an issue lay bare the secret heart of America itself. Rarely are we met with a challenge, not to our growth or abundance, or our welfare or our security, but rather to the values and the purposes and the meaning of our beloved nation. The issue of equal rights for American Negroes is such an issue. And should we defeat every enemy, and should we double our wealth and conquer the stars, and still be unequal to this issue, then we will have failed as a people and as a nation. For, with a country as with a person, "What is a man profited if he shall gain the whole world, and lose his own soul?"

There is no Negro problem. There is no southern problem. There is no northern problem. There is only an American problem.

And we are met here tonight as Americans—not as Democrats or Republicans—we're met here as Americans to solve that problem. This was the first nation in the history of the world to be founded with a purpose.

"There is no Negro problem. There is no southern problem. There is no northern problem. There is only an American problem."

The great phrases of that purpose still sound in every American heart, north and south: "All men are created equal;" "Government by consent of the governed;" "Give me liberty or give me death." And those are not just clever words, and those are not just empty theories. In their name Americans have fought and died for two centuries and tonight around the world they stand there as guardians of our liberty risking their lives. Those words are promised to every citizen that he shall share in the dignity of man. This dignity cannot be found in a man's possessions. It cannot be found in his power or in his position. It really rests on his right to be treated as a man equal in opportunity to all others. It says that he shall share in freedom. He shall choose his leaders, educate his children, provide for his family according to his ability and his merits as a human being.

… Many of the issues of civil rights are very complex and most difficult. But about this there can and should be no argument: every American citizen must have an equal right to vote. There is no reason which can excuse the denial of that right. There is no duty which weighs more heavily on us than the duty we have to insure that right. Yet the harsh fact is that in many places in this country, men and women are kept from voting simply because they are Negroes.

"Every American citizen must have an equal right to vote."

Every device of which human ingenuity is capable, has been used to deny this right. The Negro citizen may go to register only to be told that the day is wrong, or the hour is late, or the official in charge is absent. And if he persists and, if he manages to present himself to the registrar, he may be disqualified because he did not spell out his middle name, or because he abbreviated a word on the application. And if he manages to fill out an application, he is given a test. The registrar is the sole judge of whether he passes this test. He may be asked to recite the entire Constitution, or explain the most complex provisions of State law.

And even a college degree cannot be used to prove that he can read and write. For the fact is that the only way to pass these barriers is to show a white skin. Experience has clearly shown that the existing process of law cannot overcome systematic and ingenious discrimination. No law that we now have on the books, and I have helped to put three of them there, can insure the right to vote when local officials are determined to deny it. In such a case, our duty must be clear to all of us. The Constitution says that no person shall be kept from voting because of his race or his color.

… Wednesday, I will send to Congress a law designed to eliminate illegal barriers to the right to vote. …This bill will strike down restrictions to voting in all elections, federal, state, and local, which have been used to deny Negroes the right to vote.

… But even if we pass this bill the battle will not be over. What happened in Selma is part of a far larger movement which reaches into every section and state of America. It is the effort of American Negroes to secure for themselves the full blessings of American life. Their cause must be our cause too. Because it's not just Negroes, but really it's all of us, who must overcome the crippling legacy of bigotry and injustice.

And we shall overcome.

As a man whose roots go deeply into Southern soil, I know how agonizing racial feelings are. I know how difficult it is to reshape the attitudes and the structure of our society. But a century has passed—more than 100 years—since the Negro was freed. And he is not fully free tonight. It was more than 100 years ago that Abraham Lincoln—a great President of another party—signed the Emancipation Proclamation. But emancipation is a proclamation and not a fact.

"These are the enemies: poverty, ignorance, disease."

A century has passed—more than 100 years—since equality was promised, and yet the Negro is not equal. A century has passed since the day of promise, and the promise is unkept. The time of justice has now come, and I tell you that I believe sincerely that no force can hold it back. It is right in the eyes of man and God that it should come, and when it does, I think that day will brighten the lives of every American. For Negroes are not the only victims. How many white children have gone uneducated? How many white families have lived in stark poverty? How many white lives have been scarred by fear, because we wasted energy and our substance to maintain the barriers of hatred and terror?

And so I say to all of you here and to all in the nation tonight that those who appeal to you to hold on to the past do so at the cost of denying you your future. This great rich, restless country can offer opportunity and education and hope to all—all, black and white, North and South, sharecropper and city dweller. These are the enemies: poverty, ignorance, disease. They are our enemies, not our fellow man, not our neighbor.

And these enemies too—poverty, disease, and ignorance—we shall overcome.

"You can't hate the roots of a tree, and not hate the tree."

Malcolm X

Detroit, 14 February 1965

M alcolm X, the black nationalist leader, gave inspiring and powerful speeches, full of strong imagery and cogent reasoning. A week after he delivered this speech, Malcolm X was murdered by a member of the Nation of Islam, a group in which he had once been a leading figure. However, in 1964 Malcolm X had changed his position on how to achieve black goals and become a figure of hate for his former organization.

This change of heart was the last of many radical changes during Malcolm X's short but highly influential life. Born in Nebraska in 1925 as Malcolm Little, his father was a Baptist minister. While Malcolm was still young his family moved several times because of threats from the Ku Klux Klan, who burned down the family home in Michigan and, when Little was six, murdered his father.

Little's mother became mentally ill and the family of eight children was split up. Little left school at 15 and went to live with his sister in Boston where he became involved in criminal activities. In 1946 he was jailed for drug-pushing and burglary. In prison he was drawn to the philosophy of the Nation of Islam movement, led by Elijah Muhammad.

On his release in 1953 Little joined the movement. He studied personally with Muhammad and by 1954 was leader of the mosque in Harlem. He changed his name to Malcolm X, symbolizing his new life as an "ex-smoker, ex-drinker, ex-Christian, ex-slave." During the next ten years he promoted the Nation of Islam, becoming their most powerful spokesperson. However, his extreme ideas frightened many whites and were out of keeping with the views of black civil rights leaders then advocating non-violent resistance. The Nation of Islam wanted black separatism, and taught that blacks should vigorously defend themselves in the face of white violence.

In 1964, Malcolm X visited Mecca. He converted to orthodox Islam and revised his ideas about relations between blacks and whites. On his return he founded the Organization of Afro-American Unity and held meetings in Harlem to promote its policies. He was preaching at Harlem's Audubon Ballroom when he was killed.

Born 19 May 1925 in Omaha, Nebraska. In the early hours of the day he gave this speech, Malcolm X's house was firebombed. He and his family escaped but, as the photograph on page 145 shows, the house was largely destroyed. Exhausted, and wearing clothes he had grabbed at random as he left the burning building, Malcolm X kept his appointment to speak in Detroit. "More African than American," which illustrates his later belief in the principle of racial unity, was given to a full audience, despite the local media's refusal to report his appearance. It was the last speech he gave. Murdered 21 February 1965 in Harlem, New York.

I am not a racist in any form whatsoever. I don't believe in any form of racism. I don't believe in any form of discrimination or segregation. I believe in Islam.

… Elijah Muhammad had taught us that the white man could not enter into Mecca in Arabia and all of us who followed him, we believed it … When I got over there and went to Mecca and saw these people who were blond and blue-eyed and pale-skinned and all those things, I said "Well," but watched them closely. And I noticed that though they were white, and they would call themselves white, there was a difference between them and the white ones over here. And that basic difference was this: In Asia or the Arab world or in Africa, where the Muslims are, if you find one who says he's white, all he's doing is using an adjective to describe something that's incidental about him, one of his incidental characteristics; there is nothing else to it, he's just white.

But when you get the white man over here in America and he says he's white, he means something else. You can listen to the sound of his voice—when he says he's white, he means he's boss. That's right. That's what white means in this language. You know the expression "free, white and twenty-one." He made that up. He's letting you know that white means free, boss. He's up there, so that when he says he's white he has a little different sound in his voice. I know you know what I'm talking about …

Despite the fact that I saw that Islam was a religious brotherhood, I also had to face reality. And when I got back into this American society, I'm not in a society that practices brotherhood. I'm in a society that might preach it on Sunday, but they don't practice it on any day. America is a society where there is no brotherhood. This society is controlled primarily by the racists and segregationists who are from Washington, DC, in positions of power.

… Now what effect does the struggle over Africa have on us? Why should the black man in America concern himself since he's been away from the African continent for three or four hundred years? Why should we concern ourselves? What impact does what happens to them have upon us? Number one, you have to realize that up until 1959 Africa was dominated by the colonial powers. Having complete control over Africa, the colonial powers of Europe projected the image of Africa negatively. They always project Africa in a negative light: jungle savages, cannibals, nothing civilized. Why then naturally it was so negative that it was negative to you and me, and you and I began to hate it.

We didn't want anybody telling us anything about Africa, much less calling us Africans. In hating Africa and in hating the Africans, we ended up hating ourselves, without even realizing it. Because you can't hate the roots of a tree, and not hate the tree. You can't hate your origin and not end up hating yourself. You can't hate Africa and not hate yourself.

You show me one of these people over here who has been thoroughly brainwashed and has a negative attitude toward himself. You can't have a positive attitude toward yourself and a negative attitude toward Africa at the same time. To the same degree that your understanding of and attitude toward Africa become positive, you'll find your understanding of and your attitude toward yourself will also become positive. And this is what the white man knows. So they very skillfully make you and me hate our African identity, our African characteristics.

"Deep within the subconscious of the black man in this country, he is still more African than he is American."

… One of the things that made the Black Muslim movement grow was its emphasis upon things African. This was the secret to the growth of the Black Muslim movement. African blood, African origin, African culture, African ties. And you'd be surprised—we discovered that deep within the subconscious of the black man in this country, he is still more African than he is American. He thinks that he's more American than African, because the man is jiving him, the man is brainwashing him every day.

… Just because you're in this country doesn't make you an American. No, you've got to go farther than that before you can become an American. You've got to enjoy the fruits of Americanism. You haven't enjoyed those fruits. You've enjoyed the thorns. You've enjoyed the thistles.

… I say again that I am not a racist. I don't believe in any form of segregation or anything like that. I'm for brotherhood for everybody, but I don't believe in forcing brotherhood upon people who don't want it. Let us practice brotherhood among ourselves, and then if others want to practice brotherhood with us, we're for practicing it with them also. But I don't think that we should run around trying to love somebody who doesn't love us.

"I will not disgrace my religion, my people or myself."

Muhammad Ali

On refusing to fight in Vietnam, July 1967

Cassius Marcellus Clay Jr began boxing at 12. Between the ages of 14 and 18 he won 100 out of the 108 matches he fought as an amateur. After winning the national Golden Gloves heavyweight title, he represented the United States at the 1960 Olympics, becoming the light heavyweight gold medalist.

His early professional career coincided with the advent of international satellite television, and Clay was quick to exploit the medium. Big, brash, and beautiful, he played naturally to the cameras, reciting spontaneous verses and turning memorable phrases: he would "float like a butterfly, sting like a bee" in the ring. He stated openly that he was "the greatest," and was given to predicting accurately the round in which he would knock out his opponent. In February 1964 he was matched against the world heavyweight champion, Sonny Liston, the most powerful and intimidating boxer of the time. In a historic upset, Clay beat him.

Born 17 January 1942 in Louisville, Kentucky. World heavyweight boxing champion Muhammad Ali was a hero to young black Americans in the 1960s. His opposition to the Vietnam War, and his refusal to be inducted into the army on religious grounds, drew international attention. Questioned by a television journalist in July 1967, he gave this spontaneous statement about why he refused the draft. Many despised him for his stand but others felt that he was punished excessively, receiving the harshest possible sentence for draft evasion. When his conviction was reversed, Ali resumed his boxing career. He became a role model around the world.

He had a very individual style. Holding his hands unusually low at his sides, rather than high to defend his face, as most boxers do, Clay had exceptionally fast reflexes, superb coordination and excellent defensive skills. He relied on his reach of 80 inches to keep him away from his opponent's blows, and became known for his graceful dancer-like movements, extremely precise punching, great speed, and courage.

Clay's dramatic conversion to Islam immediately after the Liston fight drew further attention to the rising star. He stated that he would be known as Muhammad Ali and his new name was never far from the headlines. Ali was the best-known athlete in the world during the 1960s and 70s. He successfully defended his title nine times between 1965 and 1977 and was recognized the world over as the definitive champion after beating the World Boxing Association champion Ernie Terrell on points over 15 rounds in February 1967.

Ali's stand over the Vietnam War was consistent with his earlier statement, "I ain't got no quarrel with them Vietcong." The extreme action taken against him raised his standing and linked him irrevocably with the black civil rights cause. He was criminally indicted, and stripped of his championship belt and his license to box, as well as being sentenced to five years in prison, although he remained free on bail. However, it was four years before his conviction was overturned by the Supreme Court.

In 1970 Ali was allowed to return to boxing. No longer as fast after three-and-a-half years out of the ring, Ali lost his first major fight to Joe Frazier, who had become heavyweight champion in his absence. However, on their next meeting Ali beat Frazier and went on to beat George Foreman in 1974 to regain the heavyweight title. Immensely popular, Ali continued to fight, although his skills began to decline. He retired in 1979, made a brief disappointing comeback and went into retirement for good in 1981. In the 1980s he was named in an international poll as "the most famous man in the world."

In 1984 Ali revealed that he had developed Parkinson's Disease from boxing injuries to his head. He continues to travel and make public appearances to support sporting and political initiatives, and to raise awareness of his illness. In 1996 he was chosen to light the Olympic flame at the start of the 24th Olympiad in Atlanta, Georgia. His appearance confirmed his continued status as a world sporting hero.

Why should they ask me to put on a uniform and go 10,000 miles from home and drop bombs and bullets on brown people in Vietnam while so-called Negro people in Louisville are treated like dogs and denied simple human rights? No, I'm not going 10,000 miles from home to help murder and burn another poor

"I have said it once and I will say it again. The real enemy of my people is here."

nation simply to continue the domination of white slave masters of the darker people the world over. This is the day when such evils must come to an end. I have been warned that to take such a stand would cost me millions of dollars. But I have said it once and I will say it again. The real enemy of my people is here. I will not disgrace my religion, my people, or myself by becoming a tool to enslave those who are fighting for their own justice, freedom, and equality. If I thought the war was going to bring freedom and equality to 22 million of my people, they wouldn't have to draft me, I'd join tomorrow. I have nothing to lose by standing up for my beliefs. So I'll go to jail, so what? We've been in jail for 400 years.

"I have some very sad news for all of you."

Robert F. Kennedy

Speech in Indianapolis, Indiana, 4 April 1968

Robert F. Kennedy grew up combative, aggressive, and devoted to his older brother John F. Kennedy. After managing his brother's senatorial campaign in 1952 and the presidential campaign in 1960, Robert became Attorney General in President Kennedy's cabinet (1961–4). His role was in many respects far greater, however, since he was the President's closest adviser on all areas of domestic and foreign policy. During his time as Attorney General he stepped up the enforcement of civil rights laws.

During his early legal career, Kennedy worked for the infamous Joseph McCarthy Subcommittee on Investigations and exposed the corruption of Teamster Union Official James Hoffa. However, after 1965, when he had become a Senator himself, he identified increasingly with the needs of oppressed minorities, including African-Americans, Native Americans, immigrants and the poor, and became a sharp critic of the Vietnam War. Kennedy's forceful, idealistic, and attractive personality helped forge a broad alliance of young people, blacks, professionals, and blue-collar workers. In 1968, despite initial reluctance, he agreed to stand as the candidate for the Democratic presidential nomination.

Born 20 November 1925 in Boston, Massachusetts.

On 4 April 1968 Senator Robert F. Kennedy was due to address a presidential campaign rally in Indianapolis. On arrival he learned that Martin Luther King Jr had been murdered. Ignoring advice to cancel his visit, Kennedy broke the news to a large gathering of African-Americans who had not heard about King's death. In his emotional, impromptu speech Kennedy appealed for reconciliation rather than retribution. Although there were riots in many cities following King's murder, Indianapolis stayed quiet.

Assassinated 6 June 1968 in Los Angeles, California.

Although he was unprepared to deliver the news of Martin Luther King's death, Robert Kennedy was in many ways the right person to do so. He was a powerful orator, like King himself, and his vision for civil rights had made him the focus for the hopes of young liberal democrats, including many African-Americans. At the time, there were widespread rumors that Kennedy would ask King to run for Vice-President in his presidential campaign. Furthermore, only five years earlier Kennedy's own life had been devastated by the assassination of his much-loved brother. As we now know, Kennedy was himself to be murdered barely three months later.

In his presidential campaign, Kennedy won five out of the six primaries he entered. On the night of the victorious California primary on 6 June 1968, he was shot by Sirhan Sirhan, a Jordanian immigrant who objected to his pro-Israeli sympathies. He was 42, the father of 11 children, the last born posthumously. At a funeral mass held at St Patrick's Cathedral in New York City on 8 June, his brother Senator Edward Kennedy gave the euology. He asked for Robert to be remembered "simply as a good and decent man, who saw wrong and tried to right it, saw suffering and tried to heal it, saw war and tried to stop it." Following the mass, Kennedy's body was taken to Washington, DC, where he was buried in Arlington National Cemetery, near his brother.

Ladies and gentlemen, I'm only going to talk to you just for a minute or so this evening, because I have some very sad news for all of you, and, I think, sad news for all of our fellow citizens, and people who love peace all over the world, and that is that Martin Luther King was shot and was killed tonight in Memphis, Tennessee.

Martin Luther King dedicated his life to love and to justice between fellow human beings. He died in the cause of that effort. In this difficult day, in this difficult time for the United States, it's perhaps well to ask what kind of a nation we are and what direction we want to move in. For those of you who are black— considering the evidence evidently is that there were white people who were responsible—you can be filled with bitterness, and with hatred, and a desire for revenge.

We can move in that direction as a country, in greater polarization—black people amongst blacks, and white amongst whites, filled with hatred toward one another. Or we can make an effort, as Martin Luther King did, to understand, and to comprehend, and replace that violence, that stain of bloodshed that has spread across our land, with an effort to understand, compassion, and love.

"Ask what kind of a nation we are and what direction we want to move in."

For those of you who are black and are tempted to be filled with hatred and mistrust of the injustice of such an act, against all white people, I would only say that I can also feel in my own heart the same kind of feeling. I had a member of my family killed, but he was killed by a white man.

But we have to make an effort in the United States, we have to make an effort to understand, to get beyond, or go beyond these rather difficult times.

My favorite poem, my favorite poet was Aeschylus. And he once wrote:

"Even in our sleep, pain which cannot forget
Falls drop by drop upon the heart,
Until, in our own despair,
Against our will, comes wisdom
Through the awful grace of God."

What we need in the United States is not division; what we need in the United States is not hatred; what we need in the United States is not violence and lawlessness: but is love and wisdom, and compassion toward one another, and a feeling of justice toward those who still suffer within our country, whether they be white or whether they be black.

> " Say a prayer for our own country, which all of us love. "

So I ask you tonight to return home, to say a prayer for the family of Martin Luther King—yeah, it's true—but more importantly to say a prayer for our own country, which all of us love, a prayer for understanding and that compassion of which I spoke.

We can do well in this country. We will have difficult times. We've had difficult times in the past. And we will have difficult times in the future. It is not the end of violence, it is not the end of lawlessness, and it's not the end of disorder. But the vast majority of white people and the vast majority of black people in this country want to live together, want to improve the quality of our life, and want justice for all human beings that abide in our land.

> " The vast majority of white people and the vast majority of black people in this country want to live together. "

Let us dedicate ourselves to what the Greeks wrote so many years ago: to tame the savageness of man and make gentle the life of this world. Let us dedicate ourselves to that, and say a prayer for our country and for our people.

Thank you very much.

"The *Eagle* has landed."

The race for the moon, 1963–72

The space race between America and the Soviet Union began in October 1957 when the Soviet *Sputnik* became the first-ever satellite to orbit the earth. Galvanized by this unexpected technological achievement, America worked intensively to match it. The National Aeronautics and Space Administration (NASA) was founded in 1958.

Soviet cosmonaut Yuri Gagarin was the first man in space in April 1961, followed 23 days later by astronaut Alan Shepard, in *Freedom 7*. Then in February 1962 John Glenn became the first American to orbit the earth. The Apollo flights, the first manned lunar expeditions, began in 1967. Tragedy occurred early on when astronauts Grissom, White, and Chaffee suffocated in a launch pad fire. However, by October 1968 Apollo 7 had proved that the craft was spaceworthy for the duration of a lunar mission.

Nine months later, on 20 July 1969, while Apollo 11 astronaut Michael Collins orbited the moon in the command module *Columbia*, his colleagues Neil Armstrong and Buzz Aldrin touched down on the surface in the lunar exploration module, *Eagle*. Their announcement— "The *Eagle* has landed"—marked the broaching of a new frontier.

President John F. Kennedy fired the starting gun of the space race when he announced his determination to put a man on the moon before the end of the 1960s. The speed and drama of that decade's achievements gripped the world. The Apollo 8 Christmas Eve transmission was viewed by a quarter of the world's population and won an Emmy award. The undelivered speech Richard Nixon prepared in case of disaster during the first moon landing is a compelling reminder of the costs involved in journeying into space.

There were 11 manned Apollo missions, with landings scheduled for flights 11–17. However, during the flight of Apollo 13 in 1970 Commander Jim Lovell's terse announcement "Houston, we have had a problem" turned the third planned moon expedition into a four-day rescue drama. When an oxygen tank malfunctioned, astronauts Lovell, Jack Swigert, and Fred Haise had to use the lunar module as a lifeboat while technicians in Houston worked out how to get them home. With great ingenuity and determination, they made it safely back to earth.

With the end of the Apollo program, American scientists began to concentrate on producing a reusable space shuttle. Confidence in the shuttle was badly shaken after two of the worst disasters of the US space program. In 1986 *Challenger* exploded during launch with the loss of all seven astronauts and in 2003 the entire crew of *Columbia* was lost during re-entry.

The moon is no longer a primary target but unmanned exploration of other planets continues. A major international space station is under construction and space tourism, the fantasy of many, is a reality for the exclusive group of individuals who can afford it.

In December 1968 America was reeling from the assassinations of Martin Luther King Jr and Robert Kennedy, the acceleration of the Vietnam War, and rioting in university campuses across the country. In Europe, Soviet tanks had brutally crushed the Prague Spring in Czechoslovakia and rioting in Paris almost brought revolution. But none of these events could completely overshadow the worldwide impact of the Christmas broadcasts by the crew of Apollo 8, the first men to orbit the moon.

This eight-day lunar mission by Commander Frank Borman, Command Module Pilot Jim Lovell and Lunar Module Pilot William Anders took America one step further to achieving President John F. Kennedy's goal of landing a man on the moon before the end of the decade. During their ten orbits the crew of Apollo 8 took 700 photographs of the moon and 150 of the Earth, including the most memorable image of all: earthrise, a defining image of the home planet. As the crew rounded the moon for the ninth time they gave a televised report in which each man described his impression of the moon's surface and ended with words from the Book of Genesis.

Houston: What does the old moon look like from 60 miles?

Frank Borman: The moon is a different thing to each one of us. I know my own impression is that it is a vast, lonely, forbidding type existence, a great expanse of nothing that looks rather like clouds and clouds of pumice stone.

Jim Lovell: The vast loneliness up here at the moon is awe inspiring, and it makes you realize what you have back on Earth. The Earth from here is a grand oasis in the vastness of space.

William Anders: I think the thing that impressed me the most was the lunar sunrises and sunsets. These in particular bring out the stark nature of the terrain. The sky up here is also a rather forbidding, foreboding expanse of blackness.

We are now approaching the lunar sunrise, and for all the people back on Earth, the crew of Apollo 8 has a message that we would like to send to you.

"In the beginning God created the heaven and the earth. And the earth was without form, and void; and darkness was on the face of the deep. And the Spirit of God moved on the face of the waters. And God said, Let there be light: and there was light. And God saw the light, that it was good: and God divided the light from the darkness."

Jim Lovell: "And God called the light day, and the darkness he called night. And the evening and the morning were the first day. And God said, Let there be a firmament, and divided the waters which were under the firmament from the waters which were above the firmament: and it was so. And God called the firmament heaven. And the evening and the morning were the second day."

"The Earth from here is a grand oasis in the vastness of space."

Frank Borman: "And God said, Let the waters under the heaven be gathered together unto one place, and let the dry land appear: and it was so. And God called the dry land Earth; and the gathering together of the waters called he seas: and God saw that it was good."

And from the crew of Apollo 8, we close with good night, good luck, a Merry Christmas, and God bless all of you—all of you on the good Earth.

By the time Neil Armstrong and Buzz Aldrin touched down in a crater in the Sea of Tranquillity on the surface of the moon, televised broadcasts from space were no longer a novelty. The first moon walk was scheduled for daytime viewing in the US but on the other side of the world people sat up long into the night to see Neil Armstrong leave the *Eagle* and take the first extraterrestrial footstep. Armstrong had prepared in advance the words he wanted to speak as he set foot on the moon: a brief, solemn phrase to punctuate live commentary of a unique human experience. He intended to say "That's one small step for *a* man," but in his excitement stumbled over the phrase. It did not matter: everyone understood what he meant, and his small, everyday mistake only reinforced the extraordinariness of his situation.

Neil Armstrong: I'm at the foot of the ladder. The LEM foot pads are only depressed in the surface about one or two inches though the surface appears to be very, very fine grained as you get close to it. Like powder. OK, I'm going to step off the LEM now. That's one small step for man, one giant leap for mankind. The surface is fine and powdery. I can kick it up loosely with my toe. It adheres in fine layers like powdered charcoal to the sole and the sides of my boots. I can see footprints, prints from the tread in the fine sandy particles.

Mission Control: Neil, this is Houston, we are copying.

Neil Armstrong: There seems to be no difficulty in—

Buzz Aldrin: Oh, that looks beautiful, Neil.

"That's one small step for man, one giant leap for mankind."

Neil Armstrong: It's soft and mealy all the way down. Moving around. It's even lots easier than the simulations that we performed at one-sixth G in various simulators on the ground. Essentially no trouble to walk around. The descent engine did not leave a crater of any size. It is about one foot down into the ground and we have essentially a very level place here. I can see some evidence of soil contamination from the descent engine but it's a very insignificant amount. OK, Buzz, are you ready to bring down the camera?

The safe return of Apollo 11 astronauts Neil Armstrong and Buzz Aldrin to the command module ended the greatest fear about the mission, that the *Eagle* would fail to lift off safely from the surface and that the crew would be stranded there. A speech had been prepared for President Nixon to give to the nation in the event of disaster. Thirty years after the moon landing, the speechwriter, William Safire, recalled a telephone conversation he had with Frank Borman, who was handling liaison between Mission Control and the White House. Borman suggested, "You want to consider an alternative posture for the President in the event of mishaps." "It was gobbledegook to me and I didn't get it until he added—and I can hear him now—'Like what to do for the widows.' "

William Safire's speech, which happily was never used, alluded to the famous lines written by the poet Rupert Brooke, contemplating his own death during World War I:

"If I should die, think only this of me:
That there's some corner of a foreign field
That is forever England."

Fate has ordained that the men who went to the moon to explore in peace will stay on the moon to rest in peace.

These brave men, Neil Armstrong and Edwin Aldrin, know that there is no hope for their recovery. But they also know that there is hope for mankind in their sacrifice.

These two men are laying down their lives in mankind's most noble goal: the search for truth and understanding.

They will be mourned by their families and friends; they will be mourned by their nation; they will be mourned by the people of the world; they will be mourned by a Mother Earth that dared send two of her sons into the unknown.

In their exploration, they stirred the people of the world to feel as one; in their sacrifice, they bind more tightly the brotherhood of man.

> **"These two men are laying down their lives in mankind's most noble goal: the search for truth and understanding."**

In ancient days, men looked at stars and saw their heroes in the constellations. In modern times, we do much the same, but our heroes are epic men of flesh and blood.

Others will follow, and surely find their way home. Man's search will not be denied. But these men were the first, and they will remain the foremost in our hearts.

For every human being who looks up at the moon in the nights to come will know that there is some corner of another world that is forever mankind.

Good evening.

I want to talk to you tonight from my heart on a subject of deep concern to every American.

In recent months, members of my Administration and officials of the Committee for the Re-Election of the President—including some of my closest friends and most trusted aides—have been charged with involvement in what has come to be known as the Watergate affair. These include charges of illegal activity during and preceding the 1972 presidential election and charges that responsible officials participated in efforts to cover up that illegal activity.

The inevitable result of these charges has been to raise serious questions about the integrity of the White House itself. Tonight I wish to address those questions.

Last June 17, while I was in Florida trying to get a few days rest after my visit to Moscow, I first learned from news reports of the Watergate break-in. I was appalled at this senseless, illegal action, and I was shocked to learn that employees of the Re-Election Committee were apparently among those guilty. I immediately ordered an investigation by appropriate government authorities. On September 15, as you will recall, indictments were brought against seven defendants in the case.

As the investigations went forward, I repeatedly asked those conducting the investigation whether there was any reason to believe that members of my Administration were in any way involved. I received repeated assurances that there were not. Because of these continuing reassurances, because I believed the reports I was getting, because I had faith in the persons from whom I was getting them, I discounted the stories in the press that appeared to implicate members of my Administration or other officials of the campaign committee.

"The truth should be fully brought out—no matter who was involved."

Until March of this year, I remained convinced that the denials were true and that the charges of involvement by members of the White House Staff were false. The comments I made during this period, and the comments made by my Press Secretary on my behalf, were based on the information provided to us at the time we made those comments. However, new information then came to me which persuaded me that there was a real possibility that some of these charges were true, and suggesting further that there had been an effort to conceal the facts both from the public, from you, and from me.

As a result, on March 21, I personally assumed the responsibility for coordinating intensive new inquiries into the matter, and I personally ordered those conducting the investigations to get all the facts and to report them directly to me, right here in this office.

"Justice will be pursued fairly, fully, and impartially."

I again ordered that all persons in the Government or at the Re-Election Committee should cooperate fully with the FBI, the prosecutors, and the grand jury. I also ordered that anyone who refused to cooperate in telling the truth would be asked to resign from Government service. And, with ground rules adopted that would preserve the basic constitutional separation of powers between the Congress and the presidency, I directed that members of the White House Staff should appear and testify voluntarily under oath before the Senate committee which was investigating Watergate.

I was determined that we should get to the bottom of the matter, and that the truth should be fully brought out—no matter who was involved.

At the same time, I was determined not to take precipitate action and to avoid, if at all possible, any action that would appear to reflect on innocent people. I wanted to be fair. But I knew that in the final analysis, the integrity of this office—public faith in the integrity of this office—would have to take priority over all personal considerations.

Today, in one of the most difficult decisions of my presidency, I accepted the resignations of two of my closest associates in the White House—Bob Haldeman, John Ehrlichman—two of the finest public servants it has been my privilege to know.

I want to stress that in accepting these resignations, I mean to leave no implication whatever of personal wrongdoing on their part, and I leave no implication tonight of implication on the part of others who have been charged in this matter. But in matters as sensitive as guarding the integrity of our democratic process, it is essential not only that rigorous legal and ethical standards be observed but also that the public, you, have total confidence that they are both being observed and enforced by those in authority and particularly by the President of the United States. They agreed with me that this move was necessary in order to restore that confidence.

… Whatever may appear to have been the case before, whatever improper activities may yet be discovered in connection with this whole sordid affair, I want the American people, I want you to know beyond the shadow of a doubt that during my term as President, justice will be pursued fairly, fully, and impartially, no matter who is involved. This office is a sacred trust and I am determined to be worthy of that trust.

In any organization, the man at the top must bear the responsibility. That responsibility, therefore, belongs here, in this office. I accept it. And I pledge to you tonight, from this office, that I will do everything in my power to ensure that the guilty are brought to justice and that such abuses are purged from our political processes in the years to come, long after I have left this office.

… Since March, when I first learned that the Watergate affair might in fact be far more serious than I had been led to believe, it has claimed far too much of my time and my attention. Whatever may now transpire in the case, whatever the actions of the grand jury, whatever the outcome of any eventual trials, I must now turn my full attention—and I shall do so—once again to the larger duties of this office. I owe it to this great office that I hold, and I owe it to you—to my country.

… There is vital work to be done toward our goal of a lasting structure of peace in the world—work that cannot wait, work that I must do.

"This office is a sacred trust and I am determined to be worthy of that trust."

… There is also vital work to be done right here in America: to ensure prosperity, and that means a good job for everyone who wants to work; to control inflation, that I know worries every housewife, everyone who tries to balance a family budget in America; to set in motion new and better ways of ensuring progress toward a better life for all Americans.

When I think of this office—of what it means—I think of all the things that I want to accomplish for this Nation, of all the things I want to accomplish for you.

On Christmas Eve, during my terrible personal ordeal of the renewed bombing of North Vietnam, which after 12 years of war finally helped to bring America peace with honor, I sat down just before midnight. I wrote out some of my goals for my second term as President. Let me read them to you:

To make it possible for our children, and for our children's children, to live in a world of peace.

To make this country be more than ever a land of opportunity—of equal opportunity, full opportunity for every American.

"There is vital work to be done … work that cannot wait, work that I must do."

To provide jobs for all who can work, and generous help for those who cannot work.

To establish a climate of decency and civility, in which each person respects the feelings and the dignity and the God-given rights of his neighbor.

To make this a land in which each person can dare to dream, can live his dreams—not in fear, but in hope—proud of his community, proud of his country, proud of what America has meant to himself and to the world.

These are great goals. I believe we can, we must work for them. We can achieve them. But we cannot achieve these goals unless we dedicate ourselves to another goal.

We must maintain the integrity of the White House, and that integrity must be real, not transparent. There can be no whitewash at the White House.

"The difficult
decisions always
come to this desk."

Gerald Ford
Address to the nation, 8 September 1974

Born Leslie Lynch King, Gerald Ford's parents divorced when he was a baby and his mother remarried Gerald R. Ford, who gave Leslie his own name. Ford was raised in Grand Rapids, Michigan, and played football for Michigan University, where he was voted the team's most valuable player in 1934. However, he turned down the chance to play professionally and put himself through Yale Law School by working part-time as a football and boxing coach. During World War II he served in the South Pacific.

In 1948 Ford married and entered the Republican Primary in Michigan, easily winning election to the House of Representatives, where he was a member for 24 years. Known for his fairness, honesty, and openness, Ford was well liked and in 1965 became House minority leader. He was an obvious choice for Vice-President in 1973 when Spiro Agnew, Nixon's original Vice-President, resigned. Ford campaigned widely on Nixon's behalf, attempting to deflect and limit criticism of the President as the Watergate scandal grew.

Born 14 July 1913 in Omaha, Nebraska. Gerald Ford had the task of restoring confidence in the presidency, which his predecessor, Richard Nixon, had brought into disrepute following the Watergate scandal. However, his decision a month after taking office to grant a full pardon to Nixon caused national uproar. Hoping to avoid an outbreak of press fury, Ford made the televised address on a Sunday morning. Although his announcement drew a line under the deeply unsettling events of the previous two years, the taint of Watergate cost him re-election in 1976.

After Nixon's resignation, Ford became President. He faced a number of problems on assuming office: a depressed economy, energy shortages, and Vietnam. He retained Henry Kissinger as Secretary of State, appointed Nelson Rockefeller as his Vice-President and replaced the rest of Nixon's appointees. Ford's administration was dogged by conflict with the Democratic Congress, but he oversaw the final withdrawal of troops from Saigon, an interim truce between Israel and Egypt, and talks on arms limitations with the Soviet Union.

Not a natural orator, Ford's preferred method of campaigning was personal contact with people but he had to stop this after two assassination attempts in 1975. Despite a major challenge from Ronald Reagan, Ford gained the Republican nomination for re-election in 1976. However, he lost the election to his little-known Democrat rival, Jimmy Carter. Ford retired with good grace and went on to a long and active retirement.

At his inauguration, Jimmy Carter summed up the feelings of many when he said, "For myself and for our nation, I want to thank my predecessor for all he has done to heal our land." In 1999 Ford was awarded the Presidential Medal of Freedom by President Clinton in recognition of his efforts to reunite the nation after Watergate.

Ladies and gentlemen, I have come to a decision which I felt I should tell you and all of my fellow American citizens, as soon as I was certain in my own mind and in my own conscience that it is the right thing to do.

I have learned already in this office that the difficult decisions always come to this desk. I must admit that many of them do not look at all the same as the hypothetical questions that I have answered freely and perhaps too fast on previous occasions.

… I have promised to uphold the Constitution, to do what is right as God gives me to see the right, and to do the very best that I can for America.

I have asked your help and your prayers, not only when I became President but many times since. The Constitution is the supreme law of our land and it governs our actions as citizens. Only the laws of God, which govern our consciences, are superior to it.

As we are a nation under God, so I am sworn to uphold our laws with the help of God. And I have sought such guidance and searched my own conscience with special diligence to determine the right thing for me to do with respect to my predecessor in this place, Richard Nixon, and his loyal wife and family.

Theirs is an American tragedy in which we all have played a part. It could go on and on and on, or someone must write the end to it. I have concluded that only I can do that, and if I can, I must.

"I have learned already in this office that the difficult decisions always come to this desk."

There are no historic or legal precedents to which I can turn in this matter, none that precisely fit the circumstances of a private citizen who has resigned the presidency of the United States. But it is common knowledge that serious allegations and accusations hang like a sword over our former President's head, threatening his health as he tries to reshape his life, a great part of which was spent in the service of this country and by the mandate of its people.

After years of bitter controversy and divisive national debate, I have been advised, and I am compelled to conclude that many months and perhaps more years will have to pass before Richard Nixon could obtain a fair trial by jury in any jurisdiction of the United States under governing decisions of the Supreme Court.

I deeply believe in equal justice for all Americans, whatever their station or former station. The law, whether human or divine, is no respecter of persons: but the law is a respecter of reality.

"Theirs is an American tragedy in which we all have played a part."

The facts, as I see them, are that a former President of the United States, instead of enjoying equal treatment with any other citizen accused of violating the law, would be cruelly and excessively penalized either in preserving the presumption of his innocence or in obtaining a speedy determination of his guilt in order to repay a legal debt to society.

During this long period of delay and potential litigation, ugly passions would again be aroused. And our people would again be polarized in their opinions. And the credibility of our free institutions of government would again be challenged at home and abroad.

In the end, the courts might well hold that Richard Nixon had been denied due process, and the verdict of history would even be more inconclusive with respect to those charges arising out of the period of his presidency, of which I am presently aware.

But it is not the ultimate fate of Richard Nixon that most concerns me, though surely it deeply troubles every decent and every compassionate person. My concern is the immediate future of this great country.

"Richard Nixon and his loved ones have suffered enough and will continue to suffer."

In this, I dare not depend upon my personal sympathy as a long-time friend of the former President, nor my professional judgment as a lawyer, and I do not.

As President, my primary concern must always be the greatest good of all the people of the United States whose servant I am. As a man, my first consideration is to be true to my own convictions and my own conscience.

... My conscience tells me clearly and certainly that I cannot prolong the bad dreams that continue to reopen a chapter that is closed. My conscience tells me that only I, as President, have the constitutional power to firmly shut and seal this book. My conscience tells me it is my duty, not merely to proclaim domestic tranquillity but to use every means that I have to insure it. I do believe that the buck stops here, that I cannot rely upon public opinion polls to tell me what is right. I do believe that right makes might and that if I am wrong, ten angels swearing I was right would make no difference. I do believe, with all my heart and mind and spirit, that I, not as President but as a humble servant of God, will receive justice without mercy if I fail to show mercy.

Finally, I feel that Richard Nixon and his loved ones have suffered enough and will continue to suffer, no matter what I do, no matter what we, as a great and good nation, can do together to make his goal of peace come true.

Now, therefore, I, Gerald R. Ford, President of the United States, pursuant to the pardon power conferred upon me by Article II, Section 2, of the Constitution, have granted and by these presents do grant a full, free, and absolute pardon unto Richard Nixon for all offenses against the United States which he, Richard Nixon, has committed or may have committed or taken part in during the period from January 20, 1969, through August 9, 1974.

In witness whereof, I have hereunto set my hand this eighth day of September, in the year of our Lord nineteen hundred and seventy-four, and of the Independence of the United States of America the one hundred and ninety-ninth.

"These are the boys of Pointe du Hoc."

Ronald Reagan

D-Day commemoration speech, Normandy, France, 6 June 1984

"The future doesn't belong to the fainthearted; it belongs to the brave."

Address to the nation, 28 January, 1986

"Mr Gorbachev, tear down this wall!"

Speech at the Brandenburg Gate, West Berlin, Germany, 12 June 1987

And behind me is a memorial that symbolizes the Ranger daggers that were thrust into the top of these cliffs. And before me are the men who put them there. These are the boys of Pointe du Hoc. These are the men who took the cliffs. These are the champions who helped free a continent. And these are the heroes who helped end a war. Gentlemen, I look at you and I think of the words of Stephen Spender's poem. You are men who in your "lives fought for life and left the vivid air signed with your honor."

… Forty summers have passed since the battle that you fought here. You were young the day you took these cliffs; some of you were hardly more than boys, with the deepest joys of life before you. Yet you risked everything here. Why? Why did you do it? What impelled you to put aside the instinct for self-preservation and risk your lives to take these cliffs? What inspired all the men of the armies that met here? We look at you, and somehow we know the answer. It was faith and belief. It was loyalty and love.

"Let us make a vow to our dead."

The men of Normandy had faith that what they were doing was right, faith that they fought for all humanity, faith that a just God would grant them mercy on this beachhead, or on the next. It was the deep knowledge—and pray God we have not lost it—that there is a profound moral difference between the use of force for liberation and the use of force for conquest. You were here to liberate, not to conquer, and so you and those others did not doubt your cause. And you were right not to doubt.

You all knew that some things are worth dying for. One's country is worth dying for, and democracy is worth dying for, because it's the most deeply honorable form of government ever devised by man. All of you loved liberty. All of you were willing to fight tyranny, and you knew the people of your countries were behind you.

… Here, in this place where the West held together, let us make a vow to our dead. Let us show them by our actions that we understand what they died for.

… Strengthened by their courage and heartened by their valor and borne by their memory, let us continue to stand for the ideals for which they lived and died.

On 28 January 1986, the space shuttle *Challenger* exploded shortly after takeoff. One of the seven astronauts on board, Christa McAuliffe, was a teacher. Ronald Reagan told his scriptwriter, Peggy Noonan, that he wanted to speak particularly to the children who had watched the disaster happen on television when he addressed the nation that evening. Noonan asked him if he knew John Gillespie Magee's poem "High Flight"on which she had based the closing sentiment of the speech. "He did know it. He told me afterward that it was written on a plaque at his daughter Patti's school when she was a kid. He used to go and read it. I was later told that Mr Reagan had in fact read the poem at the funeral or at a memorial for his friend Tyrone Power, who had been a World War II pilot."

Ladies and gentlemen, I'd planned to speak to you tonight to report on the state of the union, but the events of earlier today have led me to change those plans. Today is a day for mourning and remembering. Nancy and I are pained to the core by the tragedy of the shuttle *Challenger*. We know we share this pain with all of the people of our country. This is truly a national loss.

Nineteen years ago, almost to the day, we lost three astronauts in a terrible accident on the ground. But we've never lost an astronaut in flight; we've never had a tragedy like this. And perhaps we've forgotten the courage it took for the crew of the shuttle; but they, the *Challenger* Seven, were aware of the dangers, but overcame them and did their jobs brilliantly. We mourn seven heroes: Michael Smith, Dick Scobee, Judith Resnik, Ronald McNair, Ellison Onizuka, Gregory Jarvis, and Christa McAuliffe. We mourn their loss as a nation together.

"The future doesn't belong to the fainthearted; it belongs to the brave."

For the families of the seven, we cannot bear, as you do, the full impact of this tragedy. But we feel the loss, and we're thinking about you so very much. Your loved ones were daring and brave, and they had that special grace, that special spirit that says, "Give me a challenge and I'll meet it with joy." They had a hunger to explore the universe and discover its truths. They wished to serve, and they did. They served all of us.

We've grown used to wonders in this century. It's hard to dazzle us. But for 25 years the United States space program has been doing just that. We've grown used to the idea of space, and perhaps we forget that we've only just begun. We're still pioneers. They, the members of the *Challenger* crew, were pioneers.

And I want to say something to the schoolchildren of America who were watching the live coverage of the shuttle's takeoff. I know it is hard to understand, but sometimes painful things like this happen. It's all part of the process of exploration and discovery. It's all part of taking a chance and expanding man's horizons. The future doesn't belong to the fainthearted; it belongs to the brave. The *Challenger* crew was pulling us into the future, and we'll continue to follow them.

"Nothing ends here; our hopes and our journeys continue."

I've always had great faith in and respect for our space program, and what happened today does nothing to diminish it. We don't hide our space program. We don't keep secrets and cover things up. We do it all up front and in public. That's the way freedom is, and we wouldn't change it for a minute. We'll continue our quest in space. There will be more shuttle flights and more shuttle crews and yes, more volunteers, more civilians, more teachers in space. Nothing ends here; our hopes and our journeys continue.

I want to add that I wish I could talk to every man and woman who works for NASA or who worked on this mission and tell them: "Your dedication and professionalism have moved and impressed us for decades. And we know of your anguish. We share it."

There's a coincidence today. On this day 390 years ago, the great explorer Sir Francis Drake died aboard ship off the coast of Panama. In his lifetime the great frontiers were the oceans, and a historian later said, "He lived by the sea, died on it, and was buried in it." Well, today we can say of the *Challenger* crew, their dedication was, like Drake's, complete.

The crew of the space shuttle *Challenger* honored us by the manner in which they lived their lives. We will never forget them, nor the last time we saw them, this morning, as they prepared for their journey and waved goodbye and "slipped the surly bonds of earth" to "touch the face of God."

In June 1987, Reagan called for the removal of the Berlin Wall, appealing directly to Soviet Premier Mikhail Gorbachev to remove the physical and symbolic barrier between the two Germanys and the Eastern and Western blocs of Europe. Given at the Brandenburg Gate, this speech acknowledges John F. Kennedy's historic speech nearly a quarter of a century earlier, when the Berlin Wall was first erected, and deliberately echoes Kennedy's famous phrases in demanding its demolition. In the year Reagan left office, the Berlin Wall was demolished, followed by the unraveling of the Soviet Union itself.

Twenty-four years ago, President John F. Kennedy visited Berlin, speaking to the people of this city and the world at the City Hall. Well, since then two other Presidents have come, each in his turn, to Berlin. And today I, myself, make my second visit to your city.

We come to Berlin, we American Presidents, because it's our duty to speak, in this place, of freedom. But I must confess, we're drawn here by other things as well: by the feeling of history in this city, more than 500 years older than our own nation; by the beauty of the Grünewald and the Tiergarten; most of all, by your courage and determination. Perhaps the composer Paul Lincke understood something about American Presidents. You see, like so many Presidents before me, I come here today because wherever I go, whatever I do, *Ich hab noch einen Koffer in Berlin*, I still have a suitcase in Berlin.

"Wherever I go, whatever I do, I still have a suitcase in Berlin."

Our gathering today is being broadcast throughout Western Europe and North America. I understand that it is being seen and heard as well in the East. To those listening throughout Eastern Europe, a special word: Although I cannot be with you, I address my remarks to you just as surely as to those standing here before me. For I join you, as I join your fellow countrymen in the West, in this firm, this unalterable belief: *Es gibt nur ein Berlin*, there is only one Berlin.

Behind me stands a wall that encircles the free sectors of this city, part of a vast system of barriers that divides the entire continent of Europe. From the Baltic, south, those barriers cut across Germany in a gash of barbed wire, concrete, dog runs, and guard towers. Farther south, there may be no visible, no obvious wall. But there remain armed guards and checkpoints all the same—still a restriction on the right to travel, still an instrument to impose upon ordinary men and women the will of a totalitarian state. Yet it is here in Berlin where the wall emerges most clearly; here, cutting across your city, where the news photo and the television screen have imprinted this brutal division of a continent upon the mind of the world. Standing before the Brandenburg Gate, every man is a German, separated from his fellow men. Every man is a Berliner, forced to look upon a scar.

"Freedom leads to prosperity. … Freedom is the victor."

President von Weizsacker has said, "The German question is open as long as the Brandenburg Gate is closed." Today I say: As long as the gate is closed, as long as this scar of a wall is permitted to stand, it is not the German question alone that remains open, but the question of freedom for all mankind. Yet I do not come here to lament. For I find in Berlin a message of hope, even in the shadow of this wall, a message of triumph.

… Where four decades ago there was rubble, today in West Berlin there is the greatest industrial output of any city in Germany—busy office blocks, fine homes and apartments, proud avenues and the spreading lawns of parkland. Where a city's culture seemed to have been destroyed, today there are two great universities, orchestras and an opera, countless theatres and museums. Where there was want, today there's abundance—food, clothing, automobiles—the wonderful goods of the Ku'damm. From devastation, from utter ruin, you Berliners have, in freedom, rebuilt a city that once again ranks as one of the greatest on earth. The Soviets may have had other plans. But my friends, there were a few things the Soviets didn't count on—*Berliner Herz, Berliner Humor, ja, und Berliner Schnauze*, Berliner heart, Berliner humor, yes, and Berliner *Schnauze*.

In the 1950s, Khrushchev predicted: "We will bury you." But in the West today, we see a free world that has achieved a level of prosperity and well-being unprecedented in all human history. In the communist world, we see failure, technological backwardness, declining standards of health, even want of the most basic kind—too little food. Even today, the Soviet Union still cannot feed itself. After these four decades, then, there stands before the entire world one great and inescapable conclusion: Freedom leads to prosperity. Freedom replaces the ancient hatreds among the nations with comity and peace. Freedom is the victor.

And now the Soviets themselves may, in a limited way, be coming to understand the importance of freedom. We hear much from Moscow about a new policy of reform and openness. Some political prisoners have been released. Certain foreign news broadcasts are no longer being jammed. Some economic enterprises have been permitted to operate with greater freedom from state control.

Are these the beginnings of profound changes in the Soviet state? Or are they token gestures, intended to raise false hopes in the West, or to strengthen the Soviet system without changing it? We welcome change and openness; for we believe that freedom and security go together, that the advance of human liberty can only strengthen the cause of world peace. There is one sign the Soviets can make that would be unmistakable, that would advance dramatically the cause of freedom and peace.

General Secretary Gorbachev, if you seek peace, if you seek prosperity for the Soviet Union and Eastern Europe, if you seek liberalization: come here to this gate! Mr Gorbachev, open this gate! Mr Gorbachev, tear down this wall!

"No one could live long in Berlin without being completely disabused of illusions."

… In these four decades, as I have said, you Berliners have built a great city. You've done so in spite of threats—the Soviet attempts to impose the East-mark, the blockade. Today the city thrives in spite of the challenges implicit in the very presence of this wall. What keeps you here? Certainly there's a great deal to be said for your fortitude, for your defiant courage. But I believe there's something deeper, something that involves Berlin's whole look and feel and way of life—not mere sentiment. No one could live long in Berlin without being completely disabused of illusions. Something instead, that has seen the difficulties of life in Berlin but chose to accept them, that continues to build this good and proud city in contrast to a surrounding totalitarian presence that refuses to release human energies or aspirations. Something that speaks with a powerful voice of affirmation, that says yes to this city, yes to the future, yes to freedom. In a word, I would submit that what keeps you in Berlin is love—love both profound and abiding.

Perhaps this gets to the root of the matter, to the most fundamental distinction of all between East and West. The totalitarian world produces backwardness because it does such violence to the spirit, thwarting the human impulse to create, to enjoy, to worship. The totalitarian world finds even symbols of love and of worship an affront. Years ago, before the East Germans began rebuilding their churches, they erected a secular structure: the television tower at Alexander Platz. Virtually ever since, the authorities have been working to correct what they view as the tower's one major flaw, treating the glass sphere at the top with paints and chemicals of every kind. Yet even today when the sun strikes that sphere—that sphere that towers over all Berlin—the light makes the sign of the cross. There in Berlin, like the city itself, symbols of love, symbols of worship, cannot be suppressed.

"The wall cannot withstand freedom."

As I looked out a moment ago from the Reichstag, that embodiment of German unity, I noticed words crudely spray-painted upon the wall, perhaps by a young Berliner: "This wall will fall. Beliefs become reality." Yes, across Europe, this wall will fall. For it cannot withstand faith; it cannot withstand truth. The wall cannot withstand freedom.

And I would like, before I close, to say one word. I have read, and I have been questioned since I've been here about certain demonstrations against my coming. And I would like to say just one thing, and to those who demonstrate so. I wonder if they have ever asked themselves that if they should have the kind of government they apparently seek, no one would ever be able to do what they're doing again.

"I wish him well."

Barbara Bush

Commencement Address at Wellesley College, Massachusetts, 1 June 1990

President George Bush once remarked, "If I win, Americans will fall in love with Barbara Bush," and it appeared he was right. Barbara Bush became one of the best-loved First Ladies, and as her popularity grew she built on it to benefit the social causes dear to her heart. Barbara maintained that most social problems had their roots in illiteracy, which she termed "the most important issue we have." She spoke at hundreds of events, wrote two children's books, donating the profits to literacy charities, spoke about the importance of reading on the Oprah Winfrey Show and made a weekly radio show for children, "Mrs Bush's Story Hour."

Marvin Pierce, Barbara's father, was a publisher of women's magazines and a descendant of Franklin Pierce, the fourteenth President. His four daughters had a privileged upbringing in an affluent suburb of New York and Barbara attended a private school in Charleston, South Carolina, graduating in 1943. She met George Bush at a dance when she was 16. They became secretly engaged, just before George left to serve in the Pacific, eventually marrying in 1945. While George attended Yale, Barbara had her first and only paying job at the campus store. Soon after the birth of their first child, they moved to Texas where George worked in the oil business before entering politics.

Born 8 June 1925 in New York.
There were dissenting voices when Barbara Bush, wife of President George Bush, was invited to give the Commencement Address at Wellesley in 1990. Some argued that her national significance depended on her husband's career rather than her own, and therefore did not reflect the ethos of a college educating female high achievers. However, at the end of her speech the First Lady delivered a *coup de grâce* that ensured her visit would never be forgotten.

As George's political career progressed, Barbara combined the accomplishments of a politician's wife with raising their family of six. She became an experienced campaigner and popular speaker. As First Lady she visited shelters for the homeless, day-care centers and pediatric hospitals. She publicly embraced people with AIDS to demonstrate that the disease could not be passed on through normal physical contact. She also advocated a more inclusive attitude toward gay people in the Republican Party. However, Barbara's personal popularity could not secure a second term for her husband. When Bill Clinton became President in 1992 the Bushes retired to their home in Houston.

Well aware of the contention over the choice of speaker at the 1990 Wellesley Commencement, Barbara created an initial stir by inviting Raisa Gorbachev, wife of the visiting Soviet leader, to accompany her. She then gave a witty and charming speech, ending with a rhetorical twist that produced gasps of delight from her audience.

For her compassion and support of social causes, Barbara has drawn comparisons with Eleanor Roosevelt. However, conscious of the precedents established by other First Ladies, Barbara stated that "each spouse has to define the job for herself." She remains a very popular public figure.

Now I know your first choice today was Alice Walker—guess how I know?—known for *The Color Purple*. Instead you got me, known for the color of my hair. Alice Walker's book has a special resonance here. At Wellesley, each class is known by a special color. For four years the Class of '90 has worn the color purple. Today you meet on Severance Green to say goodbye to all of that, to begin a new and a very personal journey, to search for your own true colors.

In the world that awaits you, beyond the shores of Lake Waban, no one can say what your true colors will be. But this I do know: you have a first-class education from a first-class school. And so you need not, probably cannot, live a paint-by-numbers life. Decisions are not irrevocable. Choices do come back. And as you set off from Wellesley, I hope that many of you will consider making three very special choices.

The first is to believe in something larger than yourself, to get involved in some of the big ideas of our time. I chose literacy because I honestly believe that if more people could read, write, and comprehend, we would be that much closer to solving so many of the problems that plague our nation and our society.

"Decisions are not irrevocable. Choices do come back."

And early on I made another choice, which I hope you'll make as well. Whether you are talking about education, career, or service, you're talking about life—and life really must have joy. It's supposed to be fun. One of the reasons I made the most important decision of my life, to marry George Bush, is because he made me laugh. It's true, sometimes we've laughed through our tears, but that shared laughter has been one of our strongest bonds. Find the joy in life, because as Ferris Bueller said on his day off, "Life moves pretty fast; and ya don't stop and look around once in a while, ya gonna miss it." I'm not going to tell George you clapped more for Ferris than you clapped for George.

The third choice that must not be missed is to cherish your human connections: your relationships with family and friends. For several years, you've had impressed upon you the importance to your career of dedication and hard work. And, of course, that's true. But as important as your obligations as a doctor, a lawyer, a business leader will be, you are a human being first. And those human connections—with spouses, with children, with friends—are the most important investments you will ever make.

At the end of your life, you will never regret not having passed one more test, winning one more verdict, or not closing one more deal. You will regret time not spent with a husband, a child, a friend, or a parent.

"Our success as a society depends not on what happens in the White House, but on what happens inside your house."

We are in a transitional period right now, fascinating and exhilarating times, learning to adjust to changes and the choices we, men and women, are facing.

… Now maybe we should adjust faster; maybe we should adjust slower. But whatever the era, whatever the times, one thing will never change: fathers and mothers, if you have children, they must come first. You must read to your children, and you must hug your children, and you must love your children. Your success as a family, our success as a society, depends not on what happens in the White House, but on what happens inside your house.

For over 50 years, it was said that the winner of Wellesley's annual hoop race would be the first to get married. Now they say, the winner will be the first to become a CEO. … I want to offer a new legend: the winner of the hoop race will be the first to realize her—not society's—dreams, her own personal dream.

And who knows? Somewhere out in this audience may even be someone who will one day follow in my footsteps, and preside over the White House as the President's spouse—and I wish him well.

"You have lost too much, but you have not lost everything."

Bill Clinton
Oklahoma City, 23 April 1995

William Jefferson Clinton only ever wanted to be a politician, an ambition sealed when he shook the hand of his idol President John F. Kennedy on a visit to the White House as a schoolboy. A posthumous child (his father died in a car-crash before his birth), Bill Clinton studied at Georgetown University and attended Oxford University, England, in 1968 on a Rhodes Scholarship, receiving a law degree from Yale in 1973. After teaching law for three years, he entered politics and in 1976 became the youngest Governor of Arkansas, a post to which he was re-elected three times.

Clinton won the Democratic presidential nomination in 1992, despite serious allegations of personal misconduct and draft dodging. His two terms saw the longest period of peacetime economic expansion, and his administration made notable achievements in foreign policy, including sending peacekeeping forces to war-torn Bosnia, reinstalling the ousted Haitian President, and brokering a peace agreement in Northern Ireland.

Born 19 August 1946 in Hope, Arkansas. On 19 April 1995 a bomb destroyed a federal building in Oklahoma City, killing 168 people, including 19 children, and injuring more than 500. President Bill Clinton's subsequent visit to Oklahoma, at which he gave this speech, expressed solidarity and brought some measure of emotional recovery to the nation. The site of the bombing is now a memorial.

However, scandal was never far from the White House during Clinton's presidency. In 1998 he was impeached, accused of lying about his sexual indiscretions. He was acquitted and his national apology received public approval but the trust he lost was never restored. He is now mainly recalled as a President who failed to reach his great potential.

After the Oklahoma bombing, Clinton invited children traumatized by the event to the Oval Office, where he and his wife Hillary met them and tried to answer their questions themselves. In 2000, Clinton revisited Oklahoma City on the fifth anniversary of the bombing and was able to report: "Five years isn't a very long time for trees to grow, or for wounds to heal and hearts to mend. But today, like your beautiful dogwood tree on the White House lawn, Oklahoma City clearly is blooming again." He was also guest of honor at the service marking the tenth anniversary of the Oklahoma bombing in 2005.

Clinton received the biggest advance ever given for a non-fiction book for his autobiography, *My Life*, which was an international bestseller. With characteristic humor, he reflected that some memoirs "are dull and self-serving. Hopefully mine will be interesting and self-serving."

I am honored to be here today to represent the American people. But I have to tell you that Hillary and I also come as parents, as husband and wife, as people who were your neighbors for some of the best years of our lives.

Today our nation joins with you in grief. We mourn with you. We share your hope against hope that some may still survive. We thank all those who have worked so heroically to save lives and to solve this crime—those here in Oklahoma and those who are all across this great land, and many who left their own lives to come here to work hand in hand with you. We pledge to do all we can to help you heal the injured, to rebuild this city, and to bring to justice those who did this evil.

This terrible sin took the lives of our American family, innocent children in that building, only because their parents were trying to be good parents as well as good workers; citizens in the building going about their daily business; and many there who served the rest of us—who worked to help the elderly and the disabled, who worked to support our farmers and our veterans, who worked to enforce our laws and to protect us. Let us say clearly, they served us well, and we are grateful.

"Today our nation joins with you in grief."

But for so many of you they were also neighbors and friends. You saw them at church or the PTA meetings, at the civic clubs, at the ball park. You know them in ways that all the rest of America could not. And to all the members of the families here present who have suffered loss, though we share your grief, your pain is unimaginable, and we know that. We cannot undo it. That is God's work.

Our words seem small beside the loss you have endured. But I found a few I wanted to share today. I've received a lot of letters in these last terrible days. One stood out because it came from a young widow and a mother of three whose own husband was murdered with over 200 other Americans when Pan Am 103 was shot down. Here is what that woman said I should say to you today:

"The anger you feel is valid, but you must not allow yourselves to be consumed by it. The hurt you feel must not be allowed to turn into hate, but instead into the search for justice. The loss you feel must not paralyze your own lives. Instead, you must try to pay tribute to your loved ones by continuing to do all the things they left undone, thus ensuring they did not die in vain."

Wise words from one who also knows.

You have lost too much, but you have not lost everything. And you have certainly not lost America, for we will stand with you for as many tomorrows as it takes.

If ever we needed evidence of that, I could only recall the words of Governor and Mrs Keating: "If anybody thinks that Americans are mostly mean and selfish, they ought to come to Oklahoma. If anybody thinks Americans have lost the capacity for love and caring and courage, they ought to come to Oklahoma."

"A tree takes a long time to grow, and wounds take a long time to heal. But we must begin."

To all my fellow Americans beyond this hall, I say, one thing we owe those who have sacrificed is the duty to purge ourselves of the dark forces which gave rise to this evil. They are forces that threaten our common peace, our freedom, our way of life. Let us teach our children that the God of comfort is also the God of righteousness: those who trouble their own house will inherit the wind. Justice will prevail.

Let us let our own children know that we will stand against the forces of fear. When there is talk of hatred, let us stand up and talk against it. When there is talk of violence, let us stand up and talk against it. In the face of death, let us honor life. As St Paul admonished us, let us "not be overcome by evil, but overcome evil with good."

Yesterday, Hillary and I had the privilege of speaking with some children of other federal employees—children like those who were lost here. And one little girl said something we will never forget. She said, "We should all plant a tree in memory of the children." So this morning before we got on the plane to come here, at the White House, we planted that tree in honor of the children of Oklahoma. It was a dogwood with its wonderful spring flower and its deep, enduring roots. It embodies the lesson of the Psalms, that the life of a good person is like a tree whose leaf does not wither.

My fellow Americans, a tree takes a long time to grow, and wounds take a long time to heal. But we must begin. Those who are lost now belong to God. Some day we will be with them. But until that happens, their legacy must be our lives.

"The perils of indifference."

Elie Wiesel

Seventh White House Millennium Evening, Washington, 12 April 1999

Elie Wiesel is a writer famed internationally for his witness to the sufferings endured by Jews in the concentration camps of Nazi Germany. He was born in 1928 in Sighet, Transylvania, now part of Romania, and grew up in a Jewish community where Yiddish was his first language. Wiesel studied classical Hebrew from a very early age and religion was central to his life.

In 1944 the Nazis arrived and "cleansed" Sighet of its Jews, deporting them *en masse* to concentration camps. On arrival at Auschwitz, Wiesel was separated from his mother and younger sister and never saw them again. He and his father managed to stay together but suffered terrible hardship, being used as slave labor, and starved and beaten. They were moved to Buchenwald where Wiesel's father perished from malnutrition, exposure, and dysentery just before the camp was liberated by the Allies in 1945.

Wiesel was taken to Paris, where he studied philosophy at the Sorbonne and worked as a Hebrew teacher and choirmaster. He became a professional journalist, writing articles for French and Israeli newspapers. For ten years he wrote nothing about the war but eventually drew on the experiences of his early life in his writing.

In 1956 an accident changed the course of his life. Wiesel was knocked down by a taxi in New York and suffered injuries that confined him to a wheelchair for nearly a year. He applied for American citizenship and stayed in New York, becoming a feature writer for *Der Forverts*, a Yiddish newspaper.

Born 30 September 1928 in Transylvania. "The perils of indifference" was given to an invited audience at the White House in April 1999. In his speech, Elie Wiesel drew on his own experiences to highlight the plight of oppressed and disadvantaged people throughout the world. Hillary Clinton, wife of President Bill Clinton, introduced Wiesel, saying, "You have taught us never to forget. You have made sure that we always listen to the victims of indifference, hatred, and evil."

His first book, *La Nuit* ("Night"), published in 1958, recounts his experience of life in the concentration camps. Other books were to follow: *L'Aube* ("Dawn"), *Le Jour* (translated as "The Accident"), and *La Ville de la Chance* ("The Town Beyond the Wall"). He also published plays, several other novels, essays, and short stories.

As well as being a devoted supporter of Israel, Elie Wiesel has spoken out for oppressed minorities elsewhere, including the Soviet Jews, the "disappeared" of Argentina, refugees from Cambodia, the Kurds, Native Indians in Nicaragua, and famine victims.

Wiesel was appointed Andrew W. Mellon Professor in the Humanities at Boston University in 1976 and has served as Chairman of the US Holocaust Memorial Council. In 1986, he was awarded the Nobel Peace Prize and in the same year, with his wife Marion, he founded the Elie Wiesel Foundation for Humanity.

Fifty-four years ago to the day, a young Jewish boy from a small town in the Carpathian Mountains woke up, not far from Goethe's beloved Weimar, in a place of eternal infamy called Buchenwald. He was finally free, but there was no joy in his heart. He thought there never would be again. Liberated a day earlier by American soldiers, he remembers their rage at what they saw. And even if he lives to be a very old man, he will always be grateful to them for that rage, and also for their compassion. Though he did not understand their language, their eyes told him what he needed to know—that they, too, would remember, and bear witness.

"Indifference is always the friend of the enemy."

… We are on the threshold of a new century, a new millennium. What will the legacy of this vanishing century be? How will it be remembered in the new millennium? Surely it will be judged, and judged severely, in both moral and metaphysical terms. These failures have cast a dark shadow over humanity: two World Wars, countless civil wars, the senseless chain of assassinations—Gandhi, the Kennedys, Martin Luther King, Sadat, Rabin—bloodbaths in Cambodia and Nigeria, India and Pakistan, Ireland and Rwanda, Eritrea and Ethiopia, Sarajevo and Kosovo; the inhumanity in the gulag and the tragedy of Hiroshima. And, on a different level, of course, Auschwitz and Treblinka. So much violence; so much indifference.

What is indifference? Etymologically, the word means "no difference." A strange and unnatural state in which the lines blur between light and darkness, dusk and dawn, crime and punishment, cruelty and compassion, good and evil. What are its courses and inescapable consequences? Is it a philosophy? Is there a philosophy of indifference conceivable? Can one possibly view indifference as a virtue? Is it necessary at times to practice it simply to keep one's sanity, live normally, enjoy a fine meal and a glass of wine, as the world around us experiences harrowing upheavals?

Of course, indifference can be tempting—more than that, seductive. It is so much easier to look away from victims. It is so much easier to avoid such rude interruptions to our work, our dreams, our hopes. It is, after all, awkward, troublesome, to be involved in another person's pain and despair. Yet, for the person who is indifferent, his or her neighbors are of no consequence. And, therefore, their lives are meaningless. Their hidden or even visible anguish is of no interest. Indifference reduces the other to an abstraction.

Over there, behind the black gates of Auschwitz, the most tragic of all prisoners were the Muselmänner, as they were called. Wrapped in their torn blankets, they would sit or lie on the ground, staring vacantly into space, unaware of who or where they were—strangers to their surroundings. They no longer felt pain, hunger, thirst. They feared nothing. They felt nothing. They were dead and did not know it.

"When adults wage war, children perish."

Rooted in our tradition, some of us felt that to be abandoned by humanity then was not the ultimate. We felt that to be abandoned by God was worse than to be punished by Him. Better an unjust God than an indifferent one. For us to be ignored by God was a harsher punishment than to be a victim of His anger. Man can live far from God—not outside God. God is wherever we are. Even in suffering? Even in suffering.

In a way, to be indifferent to that suffering is what makes the human being inhuman. Indifference, after all, is more dangerous than anger and hatred. Anger can at times be creative. One writes a great poem, a great symphony. One does something special for the sake of humanity because one is angry at the injustice that one witnesses. But indifference is never creative. Even hatred at times may elicit a response. You fight it. You denounce it. You disarm it.

Indifference elicits no response. Indifference is not a response. Indifference is not a beginning; it is an end. And, therefore, indifference is always the friend of the enemy, for it benefits the aggressor—never his victim, whose pain is magnified when he or she feels forgotten. The political prisoner in his cell, the hungry children, the homeless refugees—not to respond to their plight, not to relieve their solitude by offering them a spark of hope is to exile them from human memory. And in denying their humanity, we betray our own.

Indifference, then, is not only a sin, it is a punishment. And this is one of the most important lessons of this outgoing century's wide-ranging experiments in good and evil.

In the place that I come from, society was composed of three simple categories: the killers, the victims, and the bystanders. During the darkest of times, inside the ghettoes and death camps—and I'm glad that Mrs Clinton mentioned that we are now commemorating that event, that period, that we are now in the Days of Remembrance—but then, we felt abandoned, forgotten. All of us did.

And our only miserable consolation was that we believed that Auschwitz and Treblinka were closely guarded secrets; that the leaders of the free world did not know what was going on behind those black gates and barbed wire; that they had no knowledge of the war against the Jews that Hitler's armies and their accomplices waged as part of the war against the Allies. If they knew, we thought, surely those leaders would have moved heaven and earth to intervene. They would have spoken out with great outrage and conviction. They would have bombed the railways leading to Birkenau, just the railways, just once.

And now we knew, we learned, we discovered that the Pentagon knew, the State Department knew. ...

... The depressing tale of the *St Louis* is a case in point. Sixty years ago, its human cargo—nearly 1,000 Jews—was turned back to Nazi Germany. And that happened after the Kristallnacht, after the first state sponsored pogrom, with hundreds of Jewish shops destroyed, synagogues burned, thousands of people put in concentration camps. And that ship, which was already in the shores of the United States, was sent back. I don't understand. Roosevelt was a good man, with a heart. He understood those who needed help. Why didn't he allow these refugees to disembark? A thousand people—in America, the great country, the greatest democracy, the most generous of all new nations in modern history. What happened? I don't understand. Why the indifference, on the highest level, to the suffering of the victims?

"Together we walk towards the new millennium, carried by profound fear and extraordinary hope."

But then, there were human beings who were sensitive to our tragedy. Those non-Jews, those Christians, that we call the "Righteous Gentiles," whose selfless acts of heroism saved the honor of their faith. Why were they so few? Why was there a greater effort to save SS murderers after the war than to save their victims during the war? Why did some of America's largest corporations continue to do business with Hitler's Germany until 1942? It has been suggested, and it was documented, that the Wehrmacht could not have conducted its invasion of France without oil obtained from American sources. How is one to explain their indifference?

And yet, my friends, good things have also happened in this traumatic century: the defeat of Nazism, the collapse of communism, the rebirth of Israel on its ancestral soil, the demise of apartheid, Israel's peace treaty with Egypt, the peace accord in Ireland. And let us remember the meeting, filled with drama and emotion, between Rabin and Arafat that you, Mr President, convened in this very place. I was here and I will never forget it.

And then, of course, the joint decision of the United States and NATO to intervene in Kosovo and save those victims, those refugees, those who were uprooted by a man whom I believe, that because of his crimes, should be charged with crimes against humanity.

But this time, the world was not silent. This time, we do respond. This time, we intervene.

Does it mean that we have learned from the past? Does it mean that society has changed? Has the human being become less indifferent and more human? Have we really learned from our experiences? Are we less insensitive to the plight of victims of ethnic cleansing and other forms of injustices in places near and far? Is today's justified intervention in Kosovo, led by you, Mr President, a lasting warning that never again will the deportation, the terrorization of children and their parents, be allowed anywhere in the world? Will it discourage other dictators in other lands to do the same?

What about the children? Oh, we see them on television, we read about them in the papers, and we do so with a broken heart. Their fate is always the most tragic, inevitably. When adults wage war, children perish. We see their faces, their eyes. Do we hear their pleas? Do we feel their pain, their agony? Every minute one of them dies of disease, violence, famine.

Some of them—so many of them—could be saved.

And so, once again, I think of the young Jewish boy from the Carpathian Mountains. He has accompanied the old man I have become throughout these years of quest and struggle. And together we walk towards the new millennium, carried by profound fear and extraordinary hope.

"We stand together to win the war against terrorism."

George W. Bush

Address to the nation, 11 September 2001

George Walker Bush (known as George W. Bush to distinguish him from his father, former President George Bush) studied at the Philips Andover Academy in Massachusetts and then at Yale University, graduating with a bachelor's degree in 1968. He joined the Texas Air National Guard where he learned to fly fighter jets and reached the rank of lieutenant. From 1972 to 1975 he attended Harvard Business School, then went into the oil business, forming an oil and gas exploration company, "Arbusto" (a pun, using the Spanish word for bush). In 1977 he married Laura Welch: their twin daughters, Barbara and Jenna, were born in 1981.

In July 1986 Bush moved to Washington, DC to support George Bush Sr's successful presidential campaign. After the election he moved to Dallas, where he became joint owner of the Texas Rangers baseball team, making a profit of almost $15 million when he sold the team in 1998.

In 1994 he was elected Governor of Texas, showing considerable diplomatic skills and pushing through business-friendly law reforms. In 1998 he won re-election by a large majority, the first Texas Governor to be elected to consecutive four-year terms.

Born 6 July 1946 in New Haven, Connecticut. Speechwriter Michael Gerson received a simple brief for the 11 September address to the nation following terrorist attacks on New York and Washington: "Our mission is reassurance." However, the President insisted on including the phrase that became known as the Bush Doctrine: "We will make no distinction between the terrorists who committed these acts and those who harbor them." He considered the attacks an act of war and wrote in his diary that night: "The Pearl Harbor of the twenty-first century took place today."

In June 1999 George W. Bush won the nomination as the Republican candidate for President. His folksy style proved popular in the campaign but the result was an extraordinarily close and disputed contest. Bush was finally declared victor following five weeks of legal wrangling involving recounts in the key state of Florida, governed by his brother Jed. He became the forty-third President on 20 January 2001.

On 11 September that year, Islamic terrorists flew hijacked passenger jets into the twin towers of the World Trade Center in New York and the Pentagon in Washington. A fourth plane crashed in a field in Pennsylvania after passengers attempted to disarm the hijackers. That evening Bush made his famous speech, initiating the "war against terrorism" that has characterized foreign policy ever since. Three days later, he gave a more measured address at a service in the National Cathedral in Washington. By then, the world was learning the heartbreaking details of the last minutes of the victims and the extraordinary heroism of the rescue services: "Now come the names," said the

President. "We will read all these names. We will linger over them and learn their stories, and many Americans will weep." On the first anniversary of the attacks, 2,801 victims' names were recited at a ceremony at the site of the World Trade Center, now a permanent memorial.

In November 2004, Bush won a second term as President.

Today, our fellow citizens, our way of life, our very freedom came under attack in a series of deliberate and deadly terrorist acts. The victims were in airplanes or in their offices: secretaries, business men and women, military and federal workers, moms and dads, friends and neighbors. Thousands of lives were suddenly ended by evil, despicable acts of terror. The pictures of airplanes flying into buildings, fires burning, huge structures collapsing have filled us with disbelief, terrible sadness, and a quiet, unyielding anger. These acts of mass murder were intended to frighten our nation into chaos and retreat. But they have failed. Our country is strong.

"These acts of mass murder were intended to frighten our nation into chaos and retreat. But they have failed."

A great people has been moved to defend a great nation. Terrorist attacks can shake the foundations of our biggest buildings, but they cannot touch the foundation of America. These acts shatter steel, but they cannot dent the steel of American resolve. America was targeted for attack because we're the brightest beacon for freedom and opportunity in the world. And no one will keep that light from shining. Today, our nation saw evil—the very worst of human nature—and we responded with the best of America. With the daring of our rescue workers, with the caring for strangers and neighbors who came to give blood and help in any way they could.

Immediately following the first attack, I implemented our government's emergency response plans. Our military is powerful, and it's prepared. Our emergency teams are working in New York City and Washington, DC to help with local rescue efforts. Our first priority is to get help to those who have been injured, and to take every precaution to protect our citizens at home and around the world from further attacks. The functions of our government continue without interruption. Federal agencies in Washington, which had to be evacuated today, are reopening for essential personnel tonight and will be open for business tomorrow. Our financial institutions remain strong, and the American economy will be open for business as well.

"We will make no distinction between the terrorists who committed these acts and those who harbor them."

The search is underway for those who were behind these evil acts. I have directed the full resources of our intelligence and law enforcement communities to find those responsible and to bring them to justice. We will make no distinction between the terrorists who committed these acts and those who harbor them.

I appreciate so very much the members of Congress who have joined me in strongly condemning these attacks. And on behalf of the American people, I thank the many world leaders who have called to offer their condolences and assistance. America and our friends and allies join with all those who want peace and security in the world, and we stand together to win the war against terrorism.

Tonight, I ask for your prayers for all those who grieve, for the children whose worlds have been shattered, for all whose sense of safety and security has been threatened. And I pray they will be comforted by a Power greater than any of us, spoken through the ages in Psalm 23: "Even though I walk through the valley of the shadow of death, I fear no evil for you are with me."

This is a day when all Americans from every walk of life unite in our resolve for justice and peace. America has stood down enemies before, and we will do so this time. None of us will ever forget this day, yet we go forward to defend freedom and all that is good and just in our world.

Thank you. Good night. And God bless America.

"This was not just
an attack on the
city of New York."

When the twin towers of the World Trade Center in New York were destroyed in terrorist attacks on 11 September 2001, Mayor Rudolph Giuliani was one of thousands who had to run for their lives. On the same day, a primary election was scheduled to select candidates to succeed Giuliani as mayor. By that afternoon, inspired by the leadership Giuliani showed in this unprecedented crisis, many people were asking for the law preventing him from running for another term to be suspended. Although this came to nothing, the public demand reflected the new respect many New Yorkers felt towards their mayor.

Rudolph Giuliani was the grandson of Italian immigrants. Educated at Manhattan College and New York University, he joined the office of the US Attorney in 1970 and became the Chief of the Narcotics Unit at the age of 29. In 1981, Giuliani became Attorney for the Southern District of New York and began a campaign to wipe out drug-dealing, organized crime, government corruption, and white-collar criminals, notably prosecuting Wall Street figures Ivan Boesky and Michael Milkin for insider trading. He achieved a record 4,152 convictions, with only 25 reversals.

Born 28 May 1944 in Brooklyn, New York, Mayor Rudolph Giuliani's involvement with rescue efforts, calm decision-making, and information dissemination gave a new meaning to the title "City Father," as he guided New Yorkers through the dark days of continuing tragedy after the 11 September 2001 terrorist attacks. Three weeks later, he called on member states at a specially convened United Nations General Assembly in the city to decide whether they were "with civilization or with terrorism." In 2001 *Time* magazine named Giuliani Person of the Year and in 2002 he was awarded an honorary knighthood by the UK in recognition of his unique role in the 9/11 crisis.

In 1980 Giuliani stood as Republican candidate in the mayoral race for New York, losing by the closest margin in the city's

Hillary Clinton. He is considered by many a likely candidate for the presidency, not least for his ability to appeal to both Republicans and Democrats. Whatever the future brings, he will always be remembered for his response to New York's suffering and his determination to help the city rise again after appalling loss and destruction.

On September 11th 2001, New York City—the most diverse city in the world—was viciously attacked in an unprovoked act of war.

… This was not just an attack on the city of New York or on the United States of America. It was an attack on the very idea of a free, inclusive, and civil society.

… The strength of America's response, please understand, flows from the principles upon which we stand. Americans are not a single ethnic group. Americans are not of one race or one religion. Americans emerge from all your nations.

"There is no room for neutrality on the issue of terrorism."

We are defined as Americans by our beliefs, not by our ethnic origins, our race or our religion. Our beliefs in religious freedom, political freedom, and economic freedom—that's what makes an American. Our belief in democracy, the rule of law, and respect for human life—that's how you become an American. It is these very principles, and the opportunities these principles give to so many to create a better life for themselves and their families, that make America, and New York, a "shining city on a hill."

… It is tragic and perverse that it is because of these very principles—particularly our religious, political, and economic freedoms—that we find ourselves under attack by terrorists.

Our freedom threatens them, because they know that if our ideas of freedom gain a foothold among their people it will destroy their power. So they strike out against us to keep those ideas from reaching their people.

… The United Nations must hold accountable any country that supports or condones terrorism, otherwise you will fail in your primary mission as peacekeeper. It must ostracize any nation that supports terrorism. It must isolate any nation that remains neutral in the fight against terrorism.

Now is the time, in the words of the UN Charter, "to unite our strength to maintain international peace and security." This is not a time for further study or vague directives. The evidence of terrorism's brutality and inhumanity—of its contempt for life and the concept of peace—is lying beneath the rubble of the World Trade Center less than two miles from where we meet today.

"There has never been a better time to come to New York City."

Look at that destruction, that massive, senseless, cruel loss of human life, and then I ask you to look in your hearts and recognize that there is no room for neutrality on the issue of terrorism. You're either with civilization or with terrorists.

On one side is democracy, the rule of law, and respect for human life; on the other is tyranny, arbitrary executions, and mass murder.

We're right and they're wrong. It's as simple as that.

… We are a city of immigrants—unlike any other city—within a nation of immigrants. Like the victims of the World Trade Center attack, we are of every race, religion, and ethnicity. Our diversity has always been our greatest source of strength. It's the thing that renews us and revives us in every generation—our openness to new people from all over the world.

So from the first day of this attack, an attack on New York and America, and I believe an attack on the basic principles that underlie this organization, I have told the people of New York that we should not allow this to divide us, because then we would really lose what this city is all about.

… In some ways, the resilience of life in New York City is the ultimate sign of defiance to terrorism. We call ourselves the capital of the world in large part because we are the most diverse city in the world, home to the United Nations. The spirit of unity amid all our diversity has never been stronger.

On Saturday night I walked through Times Square. It was crowded, it was bright, it was lively. Thousands of people were visiting from all parts of the United

States and all parts of the world. And many of them came up to me and shook my hand and patted me on the back and said, "We're here because we want to show our support for the city of New York." And that's why there has never been a better time to come to New York City.

I say to people across the country and around the world: if you were planning to come to New York sometime in the future, come here now. Come to enjoy our thousands of restaurants, museums, theaters, sporting events, and shopping. But also come to take a stand against terrorism.

"We do not let fear make our decisions for us. We choose to live in freedom."

We need to heed the words of a hymn that I, and the Police Commissioner, and the Fire Commissioner, have heard at the many funerals and memorial services that we've gone to in the last two weeks. The hymn begins, "Be Not Afraid."

Freedom from fear is a basic human right. We need to reassert our right to live free from fear with greater confidence and determination than ever before, here in New York City, across America, and around the world. With one clear voice, unanimously, we need to say that we will not give in to terrorism.

Surrounded by our friends of every faith, we know that this is not a clash of civilizations; it is a conflict between murderers and humanity.

This is not a question of retaliation or revenge. It is a matter of justice leading to peace. The only acceptable result is the complete and total eradication of terrorism.

New Yorkers are strong and resilient. We are unified. And we will not yield to terror. We do not let fear make our decisions for us. We choose to live in freedom.

Thank you, and God bless you.

Index

Acknowledgments

Every effort has been made to contact the holders of copyright material. However, the publishers will be glad to rectify in future editions any inadvertent omissions brought to their attention.

The publisher would like to thank the following for permission to reproduce copyright material:

Martin Luther King Jr, copyright © 1968 Martin Luther King Jr, copyright renewed 1996 Coretta Scott King; J. Robert Oppenheimer, Department of Special Collections, University of Chicago; Malcolm X, ™ 2006 Malcolm X by CMG Worldwide, Inc./www.CMGWorldwide.com; Frank Lloyd Wright, copyright © 1939, 1993 The Frank Lloyd Wright Foundation, Scottsdale, Arizona.

Picture credits

The publisher would like to thank the following for permission to reproduce photographs:

The Bridgeman Art Library, Private Collection/ Peter Newark American Pictures, Chief Crazy Horse (1838–77) (oil on canvas) by Lindneux, Robert Ottokar (1871–1970) p. 55; © Bettmann/Corbis pp. 7, 11, 15, 25, 31, 39, 42, 46, 50, 84, 94, 101, 110, 114, 122, 132, 140, 145, 149, 152, 162, 168; © Brooks Kraft/Corbis p. 197; © Corbis p. 59, 73, 97, 156 (1996 Corbis, original image courtesy of NASA/Corbis); © epa/Corbis p. 118; © Jim Bourg/Corbis 187; © Marvin Koner/Corbis p. 91; © Museum of the City of New York/Corbis p. 19; © Oscar White/Corbis p. 63; © Owen Franken/Corbis p. 183; © Shepard Sherbell/Corbis p. 173; © Sophie Bassouls/Corbis p. 191; © Stapleton Collection/Corbis p. 15; © Underwood & Underwood/Cobis p. 68; Getty Images p. 201; Courtesy of the Library of Congress pp. 35, 77, 81, 105.

Cover picture: Martin Luther King Jr © Bettman/Corbis.